"My one purpose in life is to help people find
a personal relationship with God, which,
I believe, comes through knowing Christ."
— *Billy Graham*

Billy
Graham

God's Ambassador

A Celebration of His Life and Ministry
As witnessed by photographer Russ Busby

HarperOne
An Imprint of HarperCollins*Publishers*

ACKNOWLEDGMENTS

The idea to publish the first edition of this book was originally considered in the mid-1980s, when Billy remarked that the best record of his entire ministry was the pictures that had been taken over the years. While photographing much of his life, I had also made it a priority to obtain tapes or copies of his speeches. Even so, I realized a book could be only a glimpse into a very busy man's life, as God opened so many doors for Billy. Although it's impossible to name the many people who helped with that project over the years, I would like to thank the late Jim Collier of World Wide Pictures; the BGEA office staff; the Montreat office staff, especially Evelyn Freeland, Stephanie Wills, Elsie Brookshire, and Dr. John Akers, who supplied and confirmed much of Billy's material; and my staff in BGEA's photo department—Carolyn Jones, Becky Johnson, and my assistant, Earl Davidson, who ran our office in Burbank, California. I am especially grateful to my wife, Doris, who spent time typing and retyping late into the night. I also thank Chris Capen, who worked with me to bring excellence to this book. Most of all, I am grateful to Billy, Ruth, and the entire Graham family for so kindly granting me "just one more picture" for much of their life. Thank you all. —Russ Busby

BILLY GRAHAM: *God's Ambassador* was designed and produced by The Capen Company in conjunction with BGEA.
www.thecapencompany.com

President and Publisher Chris Capen
Senior Art Director Monika Stout
Art Director Mark Santos
Senior Editor Betsy Holt

HarperOne
An Imprint of HarperCollinsPublishers

Library of Congress Cataloging-in-Publication Data is available.
ISBN: 978-0-06-082520-1

07 08 09 10 11 (RRDC) 10 9 8 7 6 5 4 3 2 1

PHOTO CREDITS
Except as noted below, the photographs used in this book were taken by Russ Busby while on assignment for the Billy Graham Evangelistic Association (BGEA). Note: Letters refer to the position of the photo on the page, beginning from left to right and proceeding from top to bottom.

Associated Press: 71b, 135
Bettman Archive, Ltd.: 33ab, 65, 72, 73
BGEA Archives: back cover b and c, 6–7, 34, 39, 44, 46, 49a, 52, 64b, 66, 67ab, 68, 69, 71a, 77, 81a, 82a, 107, 153b, 161c, 164c
Blau, Tom: back cover d, 59a, 61, 128a
Bruce Sifford Studios: 53
Capa, Cornell, Magnum Photos: 76, 81b, 82b
CP Photo: 165a
Davidson, Earl: back cover a, 86, 132d
DeMoss Agency: 134b
Glenn, June Jr.: 148b, 186b
Graham, Billy and Ruth, personal collection: 18–19, 20ab, 21, 22, 23ab, 24a, 25, 26, 27b, 28, 29, 30ab, 32ab. 35b, 40,45, 47, 58, 59b, 59c, 60, 62, 63, 140a, 141a, 141b, 142a, 142b, 143ab, 147b, 151b, 157c, 160c, 165d, 181a, 186c, 188b, 189e
Gustafson, Roy: 162a
Huss, Brad: 194a
I.K. Curtis Services, Inc.: 89
Impact Photo: 83
International News Photo: 64a
Karlson, Russell: 31
Keystone Press Agency, International: 70a
Kregger, Paul: 134a
LIFE Magazine – John Domonis: 48
Los Angeles Times: 149b
Mari, Arturo: 163a
Munn Studios: 49b
Muse Photo, Bureau: 56–57
New York Times: 84–85
Samaritan's Purse: 198a, 199c
Thomas Archive: 80
U.S. Air Force: 128b
Valdez, David (White House): 156
White House: 127,139, 146a, 147a, 150a, 153a, 157b, 159
Whitmingham, Dick: 36–37, 41, 43

❧ *Contents* ❧

"Billy then realized more than ever that he had a purpose, a call. His letters, which had always been serious, now began to show even more clearly that he had but one passion: to preach the Gospel." ∽ *Morrow Graham, Billy's mother*

The North Carolina countryside became Billy's refuge as his ministry—and family —grew. He and Ruth were married in Montreat, North Carolina, and honeymooned in the nearby Blue Ridge Mountains before making the small hamlet their permanent home.

Billy always credited the success of his family life to Ruth. She created a memorable and loving home for the children and a place where Billy could truly relax.

"Ruth and I were called by God as a team. She urged me to go, saying, 'God has given you the gift of an evangelist. I'll back you. I'll rear the children and you travel and preach.' . . . I'd come home and she had everything so organized and so calmed down that they all seemed to love me. But that was because she taught them to." ∽ *Billy Graham*

The largest crowd at any event in the Los Angeles Memorial Coliseum was the 1963 Billy Graham crusade, with 134,254 inside and twenty thousand more outside.

"I have had the privilege of preaching the Gospel on every continent in most of the countries of the world. And I have found that when I present the simple message of the Gospel of Jesus Christ, with authority, quoting from the very Word of God—He takes that message and drives it supernaturally into the human heart." ∾ *Billy Graham*

Once Billy understood that God was calling him to be an evangelist, he never looked back. He often said, "More than anything else, I yearn for people to understand the message of Christ and accept it as their own."

Billy's Gospel message was simple, and throughout the decades it never changed. "God has not changed," Billy explained. "His laws have not changed. He is still a God of love and mercy, but He is also a God of righteousness and judgment."

"I realize that my ministry will someday come to an end.
I am only one in a glorious chain of men and women God has
raised up through the centuries to build Christ's church and
to take the Gospel everywhere." ~ *Billy Graham*

"I am not a great preacher, and I don't claim to be a great preacher. I've heard great preaching many times and wished I was one of those great preachers. I'm an ordinary preacher, just communicating the Gospel in the best way I know how."

~ *Billy Graham*

The Man, the Ministry, and the Message

When Billy Graham was born, no one could ever have predicted the unique path he would one day follow. He was born to a typical American family on a farm outside a small southern town. Those who knew him then described him in the usual ways: nice kid, good boy, spirited, typical, average. Nothing special. Even at the moment—and there was a particular moment—when he heard God calling him, little seemed to change. He dated girls, played baseball, did his chores, and grew up. How, then, did he become the Billy Graham known today around the world? Quite simply, he did what he has asked millions to do: he made a decision for Christ and began to follow Him.

It was not always an easy decision. Being God's messenger required personal sacrifice, time away from home and family. It required the help of parents, in-laws, and a whole team of dedicated people. But for Billy Graham, there was no other choice. God called and he answered.

For more than sixty years, Billy preached a single, simple message: the Word of God. From turbulent war years through decades of civil unrest and assassinations through the beginning of a new and uncertain millennium, his message never changed. "God is a God of love, a God of mercy," he often preached. "He loves you. He has the hairs of your head numbered. He knows all about you, and He wants to come into your life and take away that loneliness. He wants to come into your life and give you new hope and new assurance, no matter what your condition."

His message was compassionate—and effective. Billy could speak to a crowd and still sound as if he were speaking directly to you. Whether he spoke to a single individual or a television camera that reached thirty million, his ministry was always targeted toward one goal—calling each

OPPOSITE: *Billy emphasized a point from the Bible at the 1961 Miami crusade.*

"People do not come to hear what I have to say—they want to know what God has to say." ~ *Billy Graham*

ABOVE: *To ease the stress of Billy's near-constant travel, he and Ruth worked hard to make their family time as normal as possible, limiting visitors when Billy came home from a trip so he could concentrate on their time together.*

OPPOSITE: *Billy always reminded people to look to Jesus Christ, not to him. He relied on God's Word to give him strength, saying, "We must read the Bible, not primarily as historians seeking information, but as men and women seeking God."*

person to make a decision to follow Christ, and to do it immediately. "The great crowds themselves are meaningless," Billy explained. "The thing that counts is what happens in the hearts of the people."

Billy understood that people needed to hear the Word of God, and he faithfully accepted that he was chosen by God to preach to those people. Even so, he was humble. "The first thing I am going to do when I get to heaven," he once said, "is to ask, 'Why me, Lord? Why did You choose a farm boy from North Carolina to preach to so many people, to have such a wonderful team of associates, and to have a part in what You were doing in the latter part of the twentieth century?'"

Why did God use Billy Graham—just one in a long line of God's servants—to change the lives of millions of people? Billy humbly served both God and people, and he lived his life by the light of God's Word, both in his public ministry and in private. He will be remembered not only as a great evangelist, but also as a faithful man of God.

"I'm counting totally and completely on the Lord Jesus Christ, and not on Billy Graham. I'm not going to heaven because I've read the Bible, nor because I've preached to a lot of people. I'm going to heaven because of what Christ did." *Billy Graham*

Chapter One

Shaping a Life

"Deep down inside I knew something was different," Billy remembered. "I actually wanted to read my Bible. I wanted to tell others what had happened to me."

It happened at a revival meeting in Charlotte, North Carolina. The touring evangelist, Mordecai Ham, was preaching to four thousand souls in a makeshift, sawdust-floored tabernacle. As he made his appeal, and while the congregation sang "Almost Persuaded," seventeen-year-old Billy Graham went forward to register a decision that would forever direct his life.

"I didn't have any tears, I didn't have any emotion, I didn't hear any thunder, there was no lightning . . . but that's when I made my decision for Christ. It was as simple as that."

That evening, upstairs in his bedroom, by the side of the bed, Billy dropped to his knees and prayed, "Oh God, I don't understand all of this. I don't know what's happening to me. But as best as I can figure out, I have given myself to You."

In fact, despite his new dedication, it took some time before Billy would fully understand all that was happening to him. It certainly didn't dull his enjoyment of life or his enthusiasm for racing his father's car along North Carolina back roads. Some even accused him of being "too worldly." Billy gave little thought to a career of preaching.

Yet he was fascinated by preachers. He listened to them raptly, and even imitated and practiced several pulpit styles in front of a mirror at home. But joining their ranks was not something he considered seriously. "The last thing I wanted to do was to be a preacher," he said.

Billy may not have wanted to preach, but the teenager was talented at it. While visiting the city jail in Monroe, North Carolina, in the company of Jimmy Johnson, a

OPPOSITE: *In the late 1930s Billy stood next to a handmade sign in front of a small Florida church. The three dollar sign cost more than the week's offering brought in.*

BELOW: *In his early days of ministry, Billy was gregarious, loud, and dynamic—and so were his clothes. Parishioners and crusade attendees liked to comment on his colorful socks, ties, and handkerchiefs.*

"My mother was a woman who worked with her hands. You know, the day I was born she picked beans all morning and I was born about four o'clock in the afternoon. In Proverbs it says 'she . . . worketh willingly with her hands.' During the Depression years she worked on the farm as well as keeping books and answering the phone because my father and his brother Clyde had a little dairy. I remember when milk went down to five cents a quart how worried they were as to whether they could make it or not." ∽ *Billy Graham*

young evangelist, Billy nervously described his new faith for the first time to his captive audience. "Jesus changed my life!" he enthused. "He gave me peace and joy. He can give you peace and joy! He will forgive your sins as He forgave mine if you will only let Him in your heart! Jesus died so that sinners might be forgiven, have their lives transformed, and find peace with God." This central theme of his preaching never changed.

For months he struggled with God's calling on his life. Then one night in 1938, Billy faced the moonlight, the breeze, and the rest of his life. On a nighttime walk around the golf course, an inner, irresistible urge caused him to sink to his knees and sob, "Oh God, if You want me to serve You, I will. I'll be what You want me to be. I'll go where You want me to go."

No sign in the heavens. No voice from above. Yet in his spirit, Billy knew he had been called to preach.

ABOVE: *William Franklin Graham Jr. (Billy) was born in the downstairs bedroom in this frame farmhouse on November 7, 1918, three days before his father's thirtieth birthday.*

LEFT: *Billy, at six months, posed with his mother for his first photo.*

OPPOSITE: *The young preacher practiced his sermons with great enthusiasm, often late into the night. By the time the services came around, Billy said, "I was worn out from preaching to those empty pews."*

GROWING UP ON A DAIRY FARM

On November 7, 1918, four days before World War I ended, Morrow Coffey Graham gave birth to a baby boy in a farmhouse on Park Road near Charlotte, North Carolina. She and her husband, dairy farmer William Franklin Graham, named the boy William Franklin Graham Jr. and called him Billy Frank.

Billy grew up on the family's three-hundred-acre dairy farm and helped the hired hands milk seventy-five cows early each morning and again after school. Though this left him little time for foolishness, he was full of energy, tearing around the farm. Billy loved the Tarzan novels and often hung from trees in the yard, giving his version of the jungle man's yell, frightening passing horses and drivers.

Folks forgave his mischievous antics, though, for Billy Frank was a charmer. One of his school bus drivers remembered, "Every afternoon when Billy got off the bus, he would reach underneath and turn the shutoff valve to the gas tank. I would go about a hundred yards and the engine would sputter out. I'd get out and shake my fist at him, but he'd only give me the laughing yah-yahs. It made him a hero to the other kids, and I couldn't really get mad at the skinny so-and-so."

Eventually his mother, tired of her son's hyperactivity,

LEFT: *Billy, age seven (right), and his sister, Catherine, loved spending time with their father.*

hustled Billy Frank off to the doctor. "Billy just isn't normal," she explained. "He never runs down."

"Don't worry," the doctor assured her. "It's just the way he's built."

Billy later graduated from Sharon High, a small country school. His grades were average, and his report cards reflected how hard he worked on his parents' farm. But Billy Frank was far from average. And the prayers of his parents—that God would somehow direct their spirited young son—were about to be answered.

TOP: *At the Graham dairy farm, Billy was up at three o'clock in the morning to help the farmhands milk the family's seventy-five cows.*

ABOVE: *Frank Graham, Billy's father, had the prettiest, high-stepping horse in town.*

"[Billy's father] was very tall and dark and had lovely wavy hair, almost black. He had a good singing voice and sang in the choir in our church. All the girls were wild about him, and when he drove his buggy down the street, he had the prettiest, high-stepping horse in Charlotte. I prayed about Frank because I wanted that man! He was something special. But at the time we were married, neither one of us could be called a dedicated Christian."

~ *Morrow Graham, Billy's mother*

A LIFE-CHANGING DECISION

The Grahams attended the Associate Reformed Presbyterian Church in downtown Charlotte. "I don't ever remember not going to church," Billy said. "If I had told my parents I didn't want to go, they would have whaled the tar out of me." But he did not rebel. Like it or not, he went along every Sunday.

The turning point came around Billy's seventeenth birthday, in the fall of 1934, when evangelist Mordecai Ham of Louisville, Kentucky, held a three-month-long revival meeting in Charlotte at the invitation of many of the city's churches. At first Billy refused to go, but a few weeks into the meetings a friend, Albert McMakin, gathered a group of local youths and took them to the service in his pickup truck. Night after night Billy attended, becoming acquainted with Grady Wilson, and later his brother T. W., both of whom would become lifelong friends and associates. Finally one night Billy knew the time had come for him to make his personal commitment to Christ. He went forward at the evangelist's invitation on the last verse of the final hymn.

ABOVE: *Billy expressed in his school yearbook that his hopes and plans for the future were to "serve God and do His will as a minister of the Gospel."*

ABOVE MIDDLE: *When Billy was seventeen, evangelist Mordecai Ham held a revival in Charlotte.*

ABOVE RIGHT: *When Billy was nine, the family moved into a large brick Colonial house. For the four Graham children, the best thing about it was indoor plumbing. They no longer had to bathe in a washtub on the back porch.*

OPPOSITE: *Billy posed with two of his teachers from the Florida Bible Institute, John Minder (left) and Cecil Underwood.*

"When my decision for Christ was made I walked slowly down and knelt in prayer. I opened my heart and knew for the first time the sweetness and joy of God, of truly being born again. If some newspaperman had asked me the next day what happened, I couldn't have told him. I didn't know, but I knew in my heart that I was somehow different and changed. That night absolutely changed the direction of my life."
~ *Billy Graham*

"Dean Minder had told me, 'You learn to preach by preaching. Go out to a mission. Stand on street corners. Be on fire for God's Word, and maybe you'll kindle a fire in your audience.' One Sunday morning, as I read the Bible text to a country audience, I came across the words *Mene, Mene, Tekel, Upharsin*, and mispronounced them so badly that Roy Gustafson, who had brought along the Florida Bible Institute Trio, laughed out loud. Every mistake I made drove me to correct it, but some of the most important ones I recognized only in retrospect."

~ *Billy Graham*

ABOVE: ***Billy graduated from the Florida Bible Institute in May 1940.***

ABOVE RIGHT: ***Billy discovered his skill for evangelism at Florida Bible Institute in Temple Terrace, near Tampa, Florida.***

BIBLE SCHOOL AND FIRST SERMON

In January 1937 Billy Graham enrolled in the Florida Bible Institute in Temple Terrace, near Tampa. The Institute emphasized individual instruction and a thorough grounding in the Bible, with courses in related subjects. The dean, John Minder, was exceptionally gifted at encouraging students, and he zeroed in on Billy, giving him his first preaching assignment.

On Easter Sunday evening, 1937, Minder took his young student to visit Bostwick Baptist Church, a country church near Palatka, Florida, and told him he would be preaching that night. Billy faced a sparse congregation of cowboys and ranchers. His attack was loud and fast. He had secretly memorized four sermons, each to last forty-five minutes. He used up all four in eight minutes and sat down.

"Billy then realized more than ever that he had a purpose, a call," his mother said. "His letters, which had always been serious, now began to show even more clearly that he had but one passion: to preach the Gospel—the Good News."

The school left an imprint on him and helped shape his later ministry. While Billy was there, a Christian leader whom he admired was accused of moral indiscretions. Billy was shaken, but it made him more determined than ever to let nothing in his life bring shame to the name of Christ. He also found encouragement in many other prominent Christian leaders, some of God's great men and women of that time, such as evangelist Gipsy Smith, Homer Rodeheaver, W. B. Riley, and William Evans, who came to the Institute to lecture and preach.

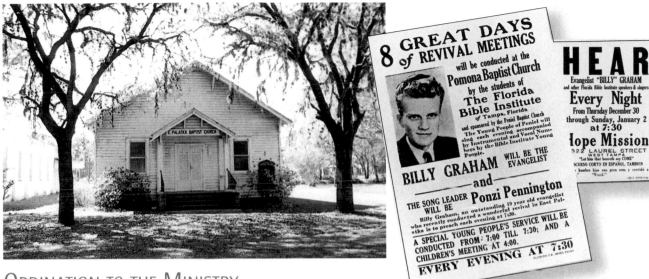

ORDINATION TO THE MINISTRY

During Billy's time at the Florida Bible Institute, God laid a heavy burden on his heart—a burden to serve Him. It was in March 1938 when Billy stopped on the eighteenth green of the golf course near the school and sat on the edge of the green. There he surrendered to the call to preach. "Oh, God," he said, tears rolling down his cheeks, "if You want me to preach, I will do it."

Later that year, Billy preached his first revival at East Palatka Baptist Church. During the revival, the pastor, Cecil Underwood, casually asked Billy about his Baptist upbringing. "I'm a Presbyterian," Billy clarified.

"If my deacons learn you're not a Baptist," Underwood said, "there'll be such an uproar we may have to stop these meetings."

That night, Billy prayed long and hard about what he should do. In the end, God led him to change denominations. The next evening, Billy announced his intention to become a Baptist and member of the Peniel church. He was baptized several months later in nearby Silver Lake before a crowd of three hundred onlookers. Billy was ordained a Baptist minister the following year, and in May 1940, he graduated from the Institute.

ABOVE LEFT: *Billy preached his first revival at the East Palatka Baptist Church.*

ABOVE: *One of Billy's first preaching assignments came at the Pomona Baptist Church in Tampa, Florida.*

LEFT: *Billy autographed this portrait to his mother: "To the Dearest One in the World to Me Mother."*

WHEATON AND A WEDDING

While war clouds gathered on America's horizons in 1940, Billy enrolled at Wheaton College, just outside Chicago. The school's intellectual atmosphere was unlike anything Billy had known before. It stimulated him—and his opportunities multiplied.

"It was no accident that my boy chose Wheaton," Billy's mother said. "He was prayed into that place."

At Wheaton, Billy met Ruth McCue Bell, who had been born in northern China. Her father, a Presbyterian missionary doctor, described her as "an interesting mixture of deep spirituality and mischievous fun."

Billy could not believe anyone could be so beautiful and sweet. He knew immediately that this was the girl he would marry. Ruth was more guarded, but soon after their meeting, she prayed, "Lord, if I could spend the rest of my life serving You with Bill, I would consider it the greatest privilege imaginable."

They were married the summer after they graduated from Wheaton, on Friday, August 13, 1943, at the Presbyterian conference center in Montreat, North Carolina. Then after a short honeymoon in the resort town of Blowing Rock, North Carolina, Billy and Ruth returned to Chicago.

OPPOSITE: *Billy knew Ruth was the woman God had long been preparing to stand beside him. Her intelligence, prudence, wit, determination, and wholehearted love for Jesus Christ attracted him to her—not to mention that she was the campus beauty!*

ABOVE: *Ruth made her satin wedding gown with the help of a local seamstress. To maintain its perfect smoothness, she stood in the backseat of her father's car during the drive from home to Gaither Chapel.*

"In 1939, before I met Billy, I wrote the following poem: 'Dear God, I prayed, all unafraid (as we're inclined to do) I do not need a handsome man but let him be like You; I do not need one big and strong nor yet so very tall, nor need he be some genius or wealthy, Lord, at all; but let his head be high, dear God, and let his eye be clear, his shoulders straight, whate'er his state, whate'er his earthly sphere; and let his face have character, a ruggedness of soul, and let his whole life show, dear God, a singleness of goal; then when he comes (as he will come) with quiet eyes aglow, I'll understand that he's the man I prayed for long ago.'" ~ *Ruth Graham*

FIRST PASTORATE

Billy had offered his services as an army chaplain just after the Japanese bombed Pearl Harbor on December 7, 1941, and pulled America into global war. But the Wheaton student was told to finish college first and then fulfill a one-year term in the pastorate.

He secured his first and only pastorate at Village Baptist Church in Western Springs, Illinois, twenty miles outside Chicago. Because of finances only the church basement had been completed, and the building was difficult to find, due to weeds in the summer and snowdrifts in the winter.

Billy was well worth his forty-five-dollar-per-week salary. Under his leadership, the church—only thirty-five souls when he started—began to grow. Despite the congregation's amusement at his loud socks and ties, they enjoyed Billy's sermons, extraordinary energy, and commitment to the church. He often rallied them, saying, "Bring your neighbors. Knock on doors. Invite people to come. We'll treat them real good." And he co-launched the Western Suburban Professional Men's Club, which ministered to businessmen over dinner. Soon he had more than three hundred men attending each month.

"As newlyweds in a first pastorate, Ruth and I were pretty typical lovebirds, I guess. We took hikes in the sunshine and in the rain, especially enjoying the arboretum nearby. On rare occasions, I went golfing and Ruth caddied for me."

∽ *Billy Graham*

ABOVE: ***The young pastor and his new wife enjoyed walking to his church.***

BELOW: ***The Grahams all came home to the farm to meet Billy's bride. From left to*** *right, standing: Melvin, the smiling bridegroom, and Sam McElroy (Catherine's husband); seated: Ruth, Billy's father, Jean, Billy's mother, and Catherine.*

"We followed Ruth and Billy's marriage with concern and interest. Concern because Billy's dedication was of such intensity that I, as his mother, wondered if he could maintain the pace he was carrying. By this time he was pastor of the Village Church in Western Springs, and he became the speaker on the radio program *Songs in the Night.* We couldn't get the program on our house radio, so Mr. Graham and I sat in the car and tuned the radio dial until the station came in loud and clear. Then we sat back marveling, and we'd say to each other, 'Imagine, that's our Billy Frank.'"   ∾ *Morrow Graham*

ABOVE: *Popular soloist George Beverly Shea became a regular performer on Billy's first radio program.*

FIRST RADIO MINISTRY

Billy's vision was larger than a local pastorate, and in January 1944, with the financial help of his church, he began broadcasting on a weekly, forty-five-minute radio program, *Songs in the Night,* on Chicago's powerful WCFL. He hired bass baritone George Beverly Shea, or "Bev," a local celebrity in Christian circles known for his song "I'd Rather Have Jesus."

Meanwhile, having fulfilled his chaplaincy requirements, Billy was commissioned a second lieutenant in the army. He was instructed to await orders for entry to a chaplains' training course at Harvard Divinity School. But Billy came down with a severe, life-threatening case of mumps that put him in bed for six weeks. He could not take the chaplaincy course, and the army granted him a discharge since the war's end was in sight. He resigned as pastor of the church in Western Springs, and became the first full-time evangelist for Youth for Christ.

ABOVE: *Ruth showed off the Grahams' first child, Gigi, which means "little sister" in Chinese.*

BELOW: *Cliff and Billie Barrows were on their honeymoon when Billy asked Cliff to lead some songs.*

YOUTH FOR CHRIST

A young preacher in Chicago named Torrey Johnson was forming Youth for Christ (YFC), an international evangelistic movement for young people. Johnson heard Billy on the radio and realized that he was exactly the kind of preacher he had been looking for.

Billy became YFC's first field representative, making seventy-five dollars a week. His priorities were twofold: first, to draw a crowd, and second, to deliver God's message. He used gimmicks such as famous athletes, stunts, and music and promoted their sessions with fervor. Soon the rallies outgrew the churches for which they were designed and were moved into municipal auditoriums and ballparks.

Ruth settled temporarily with her parents in Montreat, North Carolina. This move was a godsend. Billy found encouragement in the wise counsel and friendship of Dr. Bell, and Ruth found a valuable support system. In September 1945 Ruth gave birth to their first child, Virginia Leftwich, or as the Bells called her, "Gigi." Ruth stayed there until the birth of their second child, Anne Morrow, in 1948, when they purchased and remodeled a small cottage across the road from Ruth's parents.

Billy felt relieved that both God and his in-laws were watching over his new family. That first year he traveled two hundred thousand miles with Youth for Christ, speaking in forty-seven states to crowds of up to twenty thousand people.

During one rally in Asheville, fifteen miles from Montreat, Billy also made an important friendship. The song leader was absent, so Billy asked Cliff Barrows, a young Californian on his honeymoon, to lead the singing. "When we met," Cliff said, "Billy looked at me with a smile. He grabbed both of my hands and said, 'No time to be choosy!'" It was the start of a lifelong ministry together.

"Leaving the church left only one thing to settle: me. What was I going to do? It wasn't practical to start hiking all over the country with Billy. We broke up our Hinsdale home with no trouble. No heartache. We tossed our pots and pans into the backseat of the car and drove off. We didn't own a stick of furniture. For the first time we decided to call Montreat home. So I moved in temporarily with my parents."

~ *Ruth Graham*

"Britain in those days was dark and grimy. Food was still rationed. No cleaning fluids were available, so clothes were still dirty from the war. The blackouts and brownouts continued, so at night everything was pitch-black. Also, it was the coldest winter in a hundred years, and little fuel was available. However, the spirit of the people was not only remarkable, it was fantastic. Their smiles, their faith, and their courage were a lesson that I will never forget." ∾ *Billy Graham*

A VISIT TO GREAT BRITAIN

Early in 1946, just after World War II, Billy made his first trip to Great Britain. He was chosen as preacher on a team that did a three-week tour of England, Scotland, and Ireland to establish Youth for Christ in the United Kingdom.

Billy came home mesmerized. He felt a heavy burden for the people there, and prayed that he would see a revival of faith in the war-torn nation. Youth for Christ could not sponsor another trip so quickly, so Billy set about raising money for his return. Soon he had enough for a frugal six months in England, and he contacted Cliff Barrows and asked if he and his wife, Billie, would join him. They accepted immediately, and Ruth later joined them for part of the trip.

For six months Billy and Cliff preached across Great Britain, speaking in twenty-seven cities and towns—at 360 meetings—between October 1946 and March 1947. A bond was forged between the two men, and their ministry styles changed. Gradually they became slightly less brash and noisy, and both realized an evolution was taking place in their thinking. Near the end, Billy said to Cliff, "Maybe instead of one-day rallies, God will lead us back to our country to hold some one-week meetings. Maybe even two. Pray with me about it."

TOP: *Post-war Britain in early 1946 was so devastated that Billy felt called to return.*

ABOVE: *Billy and Ruth spent six months preaching in war-torn England with Cliff and Billie Barrows.*

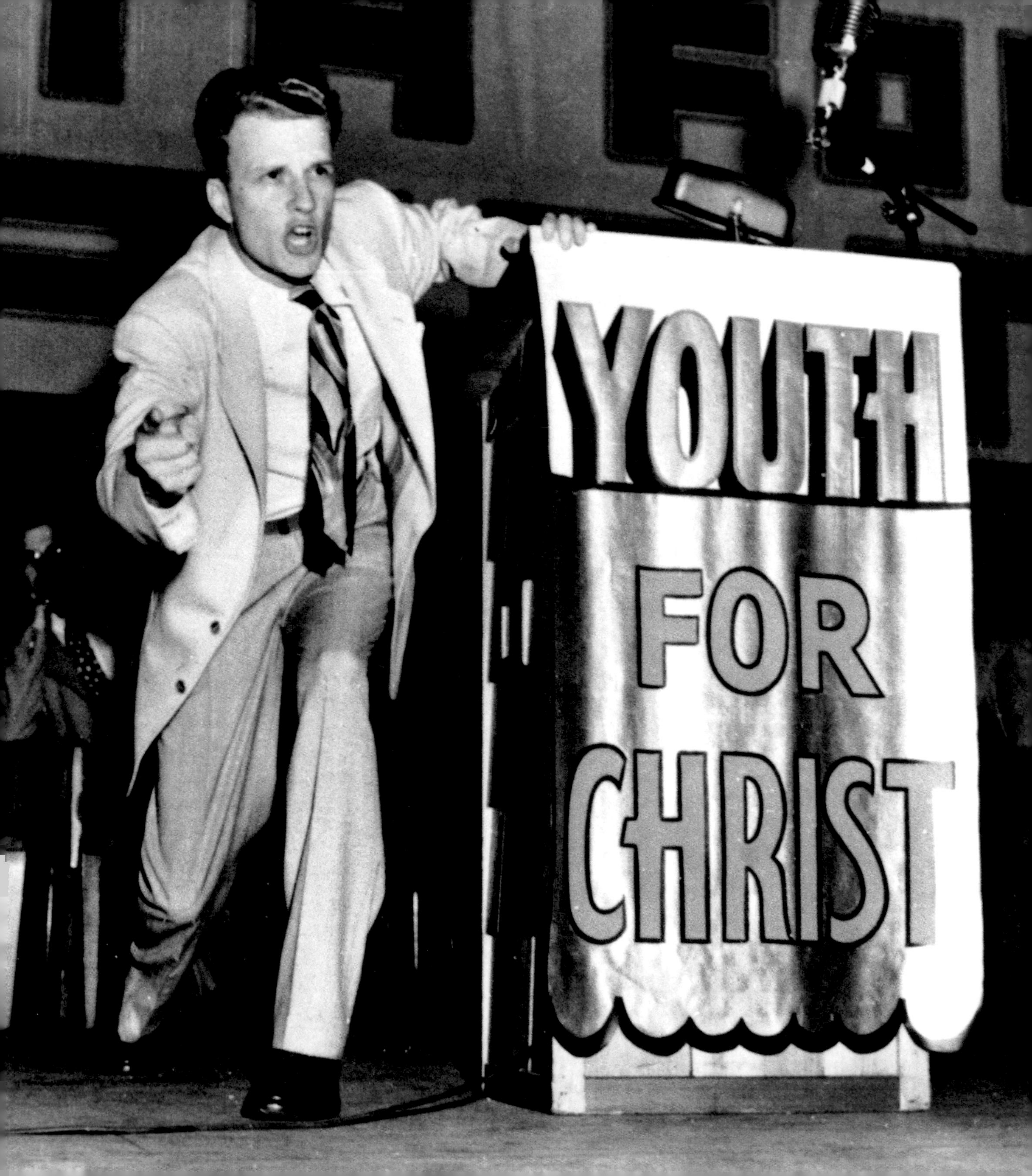
YOUTH
FOR
CHRIST

"Give him five minutes and he'll think up enough projects to keep many staffs busy for months." ~ *Luverne Gustavson, Billy's secretary at Northwestern Schools*

NORTHWESTERN SCHOOLS

In December 1947, at age twenty-nine, Billy agreed to become president of Northwestern Schools in Minneapolis. During his four years as president, enrollment grew from eight hundred to twelve hundred students. There, Billy gained valuable experience in finance, promotion, delegation, team-building—and most of all, crusade work.

As Billy ran the school, he continued to get the Gospel out to as many people as possible. He and his team—Cliff Barrows, George Beverly Shea, and Grady Wilson, then a pastor in South Carolina—started by working together on several successful citywide meetings, including one in Charlotte, Billy's hometown. He then turned the team more and more to mass evangelism, with meetings in Miami, Baltimore, and Altoona, Pennsylvania. Feeling the crush of too many irons in the fire, as the administrative head of a school, vice president of Youth for Christ, and crusading evangelist, Billy confided in a friend, "I have made so many promises, I'll never be able to keep them all."

He did keep one promise, however, and it heralded the beginning of his lifetime work: a three-week campaign in Los Angeles.

OPPOSITE: *At twenty-seven, Billy resigned his pulpit to go on the road for Youth for Christ. Little did he know that he would soon be preaching in front of thousands of people of all ages.*

ABOVE: *The Northwestern Schools campus, where Billy served as president for four years.*

BELOW: *T. W. Wilson and Billy worked closely together as the school's top administrators.*

The Los Angeles tent meetings in 1949 launched Billy's ministry. The events saw him preaching to thousands of people—a crowd that included Hollywood celebrities and other powerful people in the media.

"I read Ephesians again and again, where it mentions that the Lord gave some to be evangelists and some to be pastors. God just did not want me to be a pastor. It was time to take up what the Lord called me to do—evangelism." *Billy Graham*

A NEW EVANGELIST ARISES

BILLY GRAHAM HOLDS A REVIVAL IN LOS ANGELES AND CONVERTS 6,000 OF HIS 300,000 LISTENERS

Chapter Two

A Lifetime of Ministry Begins

In the late 1940s, Billy attended a conference in California only weeks before his largest crusade to date was to start. Some young theologians were also there who were expressing their doubts about the authority of the Bible. "Suddenly, I wondered if the Bible could be trusted completely," Billy said.

Billy began to study the subject intensively, turning to the Scriptures themselves for guidance. "The Apostle Paul," Billy said, "wrote to Timothy saying, 'All Scripture is given by inspiration of God.' Jesus himself said, 'Heaven and earth shall pass away but my Word shall not pass away.' I thought also of Christ's own attitude. He loved the Scriptures, quoted from them constantly, and never once intimated that they might be false."

Billy then recalled the moment that changed him forever. "That night, I walked out in the moonlight, my heart heavy and burdened. I dropped to my knees and opened my Bible on a tree stump. If the issue were not settled soon, I knew I could not go on. 'Oh God,' I prayed, 'there are many things in this book I do not understand. But God, I am going to accept this book as Your Word by faith. I'm going to allow my faith to go beyond my intellect and believe that this is Your inspired Word.' From that moment on I have never doubted God's Word. When I quote the Bible, I believe I am quoting the very Word of God and there's an extra power in it. One month later, we began the Los Angeles crusade."

Los Angeles was Billy's most ambitious effort to date. Advance press coverage was minimal, but that changed as the weeks passed and the extraordinary conversion stories captured the public's attention. Billy was preaching with a new confidence

OPPOSITE: *The 1949 Los Angeles revival meetings, Billy's first major national media exposure, catapulted his message onto the pages of* Life *magazine.*

BELOW: **Time** *magazine dubbed Billy the "blond, trumpet-lunged North Carolinian" in its coverage of the Los Angeles events.*

"Since my experience in the mountain woods of the conference center in California, I was no longer struggling internally. There was no gap between what I said and what I knew I believed deep in my soul. I began to sense the presence and power of God that I had not felt for months, and I have not had a doubt about the Bible being God's inspired Word since that time." ~ *Billy Graham*

and fervor and the meetings continued night after night for eight weeks. "The Los Angeles crusade," Billy recalled, "marked a decisive turning point for our ministry."

Throughout this milestone crusade, Billy firmly believed God was at work. "Something was happening that all the media coverage in the world could not explain," he said. "And neither could I. As Ruth said, 'The credit belonged solely to God.' That was the secret of everything that had happened. God had answered prayer."

ABOVE: *Billy was thirty-one years old when the Los Angeles rally pushed him onto the national scene.*

RIGHT: *Los Angeles was scheduled to run for three weeks but was extended five times to a total of eight weeks.*

OPPOSITE: *Night after night, crowds packed the tent as the momentum of the Los Angeles rally continued to build.*

6TH GREAT SIN-SMASHING WEEK

IN THE CANVAS CATHEDRAL WITH THE STEEPLE OF LIGHT

AT THE REQUEST OF HUNDREDS OF MINISTERS AND THOUSANDS OF FOLLOWERS THE GREATEST REVIVAL CAMPAIGN IN GREATER LOS ANGELES HISTORY CONTINUES UNTIL FURTHER NOTICE.

MORE THAN 200,000 GREATER LOS ANGELES PEOPLE HAVE HEARD BILLY GRAHAM, AMERICA'S FOREMOST EVANGELIST IN HIS GREATER L.A. MEETINGS.

BILLY GRAHAM

AMERICA'S FOREMOST EVANGELIST IN GREATER L.A.'S GREATEST REVIVAL

Unprecedented demands by the people of Los Angeles, and definite leadings of the spirit of God have resulted in the continuance of Billy Graham's record-breaking revival meetings for at least another week. Dr. Graham, after much prayer and at great personal sacrifice has agreed. We will not announce a closing date for this great revival. The event is in the hands of Almighty God!

SPONSORED BY

6000 FREE SEATS

THE ROAD TO LOS ANGELES

A Los Angeles committee wanted Billy to lead a citywide, old-fashioned tent revival. Excited, he told Ruth, "That's a real big city. Next to New York and Chicago, it's about the most important place in the country. They say they'll put up the biggest tent in the history of evangelism."

Los Angeles would be the first turning point in Billy Graham's career. But first there were things to settle.

Billy's early citywide campaigns with Cliff Barrows and Bev Shea in Charlotte, North Carolina, and Modesto, California, in 1948 had been somewhat disappointing. The crowds were small and the people coming forward were few. Acutely aware of the ministry's weaknesses, Billy and his new team met to discuss the most frequent criticisms of evangelism. They narrowed their list to four main problems: finances, moral integrity, antichurch sentiments, and no follow-up for the people who made decisions for Christ. Billy determined he would change these things in his ministry—and started immediately to do so.

"One day when the telephone rang it was Billy. He said, 'Mother, if you only knew how the Holy Spirit is at work here, you would come.' I wanted to go very much but Mr. Graham didn't want to go up in an airplane! Los Angeles was a world away from the dairy farm." ⁓ *Morrow Graham*

LOS ANGELES MEETINGS EXTENDED

The Christ for Greater Los Angeles campaign began in late September 1949 in two old circus tents joined together in a parking lot in downtown Los Angeles. The "canvas cathedral" held six thousand people. Counselors in a separate, five-hundred-capacity prayer tent spoke with each new Christian and passed their information on to concerned ministers. Billy talked about world affairs, preaching with a Bible in one hand and a newspaper in the other.

As the three-week campaign moved to a close, some on the committee urged that it be extended one more week. Unsure, Billy asked God for guidance.

Billy believed the sign God gave him was the conversion of a big Texas cowboy—a local radio celebrity, heavy drinker, and racehorse owner named Stuart Hamblen. Billy had met Stuart before the campaign began. Both Southerners, they liked each other, and Stuart invited Billy to be a guest on his radio show. After the radio interview, Stuart urged his listeners to attend the crusade, blurting out, "I'll be there, too!"

Stuart kept his promise, but he stomped out of the meeting when the preaching began. He wandered miserably from bar to bar, and eventually called Billy's hotel at 2:00 a.m. to ask Billy to pray for him.

Billy refused. He knew Stuart had to make his own connection with Jesus—Billy couldn't do it for him. About 5:00 a.m. Stuart did, making Jesus Christ the Lord of his life. Later that morning, Stuart announced to his listeners that he had quit smoking and drinking and would go forward at the tent meeting that night. Convinced that Stuart's conversion was the sign he had prayed for, Billy extended the Los Angeles crusade.

TOP: *Stuart and Suzy Hamblen met the Grahams and began a lifelong friendship.*

ABOVE: *A group of Hollywood moguls offered the thirty-one-year-old evangelist a contract to be a leading man in the movies, but Billy turned the* offer down, saying, *"I wouldn't do it for one million dollars a month."*

OPPOSITE: *Billy visited with a group from the Hollywood community, including actors Jimmy Stewart (far right) and Spencer Tracy (far left).*

"Physically, I wanted the campaign to close. There comes a time when the evangelist becomes physically exhausted. I had lost twenty pounds and my entire dependence had to be from God for messages and for strength. I learned that a strange spiritual law operates. Truly, God's strength is made perfect in weakness. The weaker I became, the more powerful became the preaching." ∾ *Billy Graham*

HIS TRUE MISSION IS CONFIRMED

After eight weeks, on Sunday, November 20, 1949, Billy preached his sixty-fifth sermon before sixteen thousand people, and the Los Angeles campaign came to a close.

One minister described Billy's impact on the city: "In eight weeks, he had more people thinking and talking about the claims of Christ than had all the city's pulpiteers in a year's time. When the crusade closed, we faced a community that was at least willing to talk about Jesus. My church got a dozen new members, but it got much more: it got new inspiration, zeal, and a spiritual uplift that can never be described."

God had accomplished more than anyone had dared to imagine. Exhausted, Billy and Ruth were unsure whether this was the climax or just the beginning, but they knew one thing: they had surely seen God at work.

"Dear Billie: I thank God my wife and I had the privilege of attending the tent meetings. We brought an old friend one night, but he won't come back. The reason he gives is that he does not like the way you kept your handkerchief hanging out of your pocket. I think Billie it would be nice if you pushed it down in your pocket. . . . I know thousands of Christians would feel the same as my old friend. And let all the people say, AMEN! Lots of Love, A. Scot."

~ *A. Scot*

"I had already announced from the pulpit in Columbia that I would be preaching on judgment and hell. The temptation came very strongly to me that maybe I should switch to another subject. Mr. Luce [the publisher of *Time* and *Life* magazines] was a New York sophisticate. It seemed to me to be the least likely way to win his favor. Then, the Lord laid Jeremiah 1:17 on my heart: 'Speak unto them all that I command thee: be not dismayed at their faces, lest I confound thee before them.' It was as if He were saying to me, 'If you pull your punches, I'll confound you. I'll make you look like a fool in front of men!'" *Billy Graham*

Unparalleled Opportunities

After the Los Angeles campaign, Billy had swiftly risen to national prominence. Invitations were coming from everywhere. Beginning with Boston, he preached six campaigns in 1950—Columbia, South Carolina; New England; Portland, Oregon; Minneapolis; and finally, Atlanta—logging twenty-four weeks of actual nightly preaching. That year, 1.7 million people attended the crusades, and more than forty-three thousand people made decisions for Christ.

After Boston, Henry R. Luce, the powerful magazine publisher, sent word that he was coming to the Columbia campaign; Luce wanted to meet this young evangelist. While a guest in Governor Strom Thurmond's mansion, Billy spent an evening with Luce. The two men talked almost all night, and Luce's magazines became fair and balanced in their coverage of Billy.

"I knew that this man, Henry Luce, had the power to promote our work internationally," Billy recalled. "My interest lay not in the fact that *Time* and *Life* could give us an incredible amount of coverage, but that they could spread the word of evangelism to the ends of the world."

OPPOSITE: **Life** *magazine captured Billy preaching to the masses at a crusade in Columbia, South Carolina, in the winter of 1950. The meeting had forty thousand people in attendance.*

ABOVE: *Cliff Barrows led the choir while Billy and Bev Shea joined in.*

LEFT: *South Carolina governor Strom Thurmond (left) joined Billy and his parents at the South Carolina crusade.*

A nation that takes the risk of peace will get peace just as the nation that takes the risk

The Boston

TWENTY-TWO PAGES—FIVE CENTS

Entered as 2nd Class Matter at Boston P. O.
Copyright, 1950, by Post Pub. Co.

MONDAY, APRIL 24, 1950. ****

40,000 HEAR BILLY GR
BIG RALLY ON BOSTO

Huge Crowd Braves Rain and Chill at Greatest Prayer Meeting in Common's His
Program for World Peace----Calls on President and Congress to Declare Day of
Spiritual Regeneration Needed----Thousands Wave Handkerchiefs in Thrilling

LARGEST THRONG IN HISTORY TO ATTEND A PRAYER MEETING ON HISTORIC BOSTON COMMON BRAVES INCLEMENT WEATHER TO H
This sweeping panorama shows part of the 40,000 men, women and children who flocked to the Boston Common to hear the Rev. Billy Graham conduct his final revival meeting in Boston.
mon. There was a light drizzle when this picture was made, but the weather cleared shortly afterwards, though on the cool side. The crowd gave the evangelist a tremendous ovation and he

Billy's first engagement after Los Angeles began as an eight-day campaign in Boston's historic Park Street Congregational Church. Billy did not believe that the revival fervor in the west would be repeated in staid New England.

But after eighteen days, more than seventy churches had caught the fire and three thousand people from all walks of life had stepped forward to declare their newfound faith in Jesus Christ.

On January 16, 1950, Boston Garden was packed to the rafters. Sixteen thousand people crammed inside while ten thousand were turned away for lack of seats. In April the team returned for a massive rally on Boston Common.

"These people coming forward at a crusade were not responding to a man. They certainly were not mesmerized by the small figure of Billy Graham standing at the edge of the platform. There was no fever pitch of emotion in the crowd. Something far greater was at work. In Ruth's words, 'It isn't a culture or a personality responding to a program or a man, but the soul responding to the God who created it.'"

~ *Julie Nixon Eisenhower, from her book* Special People

A NEW ORGANIZATION BEGINS

One night in Portland, Billy told the crowd that he needed twenty-five thousand dollars to go on the radio. After the service, the audience gave or pledged exactly twenty-five thousand dollars. The way was clear for a radio ministry.

When Grady Wilson tried to deposit the money in a Portland bank, though, officials informed him that if he deposited the money in his name, he would be liable for taxes. And the money could not be deposited in something like "the Billy Graham radio fund" unless it was a duly constituted organization. Billy telephoned George Wilson, the business manager of Northwestern Schools in Minneapolis, and Wilson flew to Portland with articles of incorporation.

The ministry was named the Billy Graham Evangelistic Association (BGEA), and on November 5, 1950, BGEA aired *The Hour of Decision*, its first weekly radio broadcast.

ABOVE: *Public relations specialists Walter Bennett (left) and Fred Dienert had pursued Billy for months by telephone, telegram, and in person, believing he should be on national radio.*

ABOVE RIGHT: *Billy's colleague at Northwestern Schools, George Wilson, filed the Billy Graham Evangelistic Association's articles of incorporation.*

OPPOSITE: *After months of preparation, at 2:00 p.m. on Sunday, November 5, 1950, Cliff Barrows stepped up to a microphone in crowded Ponce de León baseball park and said, "This is* The Hour of Decision *with Billy Graham!" Ruth had suggested the program be named* The Hour of Decision, *since Billy's emphasis was on people deciding for Christ. And for the next thirty minutes, the program aired live on ABC, broadcasting coast to coast on more than 150 stations.*

"Billy wanted Grady to read Scripture. He wanted the choir to sing, Bev to do a solo. He wanted me to announce, and he just wanted to preach. We all had butterflies because it was going out live. We couldn't retract it. There were no tape recorders yet. Five weeks later, *The Hour of Decision* had gained the highest audience rating ever accorded a religious program, and within five years 850 stations carried the program across America and around the world. Every crusade city became a studio."

∽ *Cliff Barrows*

THE HOUR OF DECISION AND "MY ANSWER"

On November 5, 1950, *The Hour of Decision* began broadcasting on ABC from Atlanta, Georgia. A thirty-minute weekly program, it was hosted by Cliff Barrows, with Bible reading and a message from Billy.

Listeners from almost every country and in every conceivable circumstance wrote Billy to tell him how God used those broadcasts to change their lives. They also wrote in search for biblical answers to questions on everything from religious, social, and ethical problems to marital strife and childrearing.

To help address some of these questions, Billy started a daily advice column, "My Answer," in December 1952. As he did in his own life, Billy found the answers to his readers' problems in the Bible. "After much research and conversation with psychiatrists and psychologists," he said, "I have yet to discover a source of practical advice and hope that compares to the wisdom found in the Bible."

Within one year, "My Answer" was syndicated in seventy-three daily newspapers across America. Fifty years later, it has reached more than five million readers, and its predecessor, *The Hour of Decision*, has been heard on hundreds of radio stations worldwide.

TOP: *During his 1962 visit to South America, Billy broadcast* The Hour of Decision *from missionary station* HCJB *in Quito, Ecuador.*

ABOVE: *Just a few months after Billy's radio broadcasts began, executives at the* Chicago Tribune–New York News *approached him to write a newspaper column.*

"I am a life-termer in this state penitentiary, and for ten years I have been dreaming and planning for the day when I could escape this horrible place. My plans for escape were almost complete when last Sunday a man in the cell next to me turned his radio to *The Hour of Decision*. I could not help but listen. . . . My heart was strangely warmed, and for the first time in my life I felt the presence of God. . . . I have discarded my plans for escape because I realize that God can use me right here in this prison to help others find the wonderful peace that I have in Christ." ∼ *C. J., at a southern state penitentiary*

"Many of the articles in *Decision* magazine have helped me and have made an impact on my life. Your sermons have given me boldness to face the giants, and I finally started to obey the words and commands of God regardless of the cost. My neighbors and relatives have noticed the peace, joy, and happiness I now have." ∼ *C. I., Nigeria*

CHRISTIANITY TODAY AND DECISION

Early one morning in 1953, an idea raced through Billy's mind. "Trying not to disturb Ruth, I slipped out of bed and into my study upstairs to write. A couple of hours later, the concept of a magazine was complete. I thought its name should be *Christianity Today*."

The magazine would be aimed primarily at ministers, and would restore intellectual respectability and spiritual impact to evangelical Christianity, affirming the transforming power of the Word of God.

The first issue was published in November 1956, with the generous support of J. Howard Pew, who helped finance the magazine for many years. Carl Henry, a respected theologian, served as editor, while Billy served as chairman of the board. The wisdom of Ruth's father, Dr. L. Nelson Bell, served "as a compass" for the publication as well.

Several years later, Billy created another magazine. "I felt we needed two publications," he said, "one on the theological level and a more popular magazine to help ordinary Christians in their witness and daily walk. We would also include news of our past crusades and a calendar of planned crusades across the U.S. and around the world to promote prayer support for our scheduled meetings."

Decision debuted in November 1960. By the time it celebrated its tenth anniversary, its circulation exceeded four million. Today, it is published monthly in several languages (including Braille) and distributed in 163 countries, with bulk mailings sent to prisons, hospitals, and overseas mission groups.

TOP: **Decision** *magazine has been published since 1960 and is distributed around the world.*

ABOVE: **Christianity Today** *continues to address current theological issues facing church leaders, publishing book reviews, interviews, and editorials from respected evangelicals.*

"I was saved years ago while reading *Decision* magazine; I was led to the Lord by some woman's testimony. I wish I had kept that issue of *Decision*. I am still taking part in service to the Lord. What a wonderful Savior we serve—He is so kind and patient with us." ∼ *E. B., Kentucky*

One of Billy's largest crusades during the 1950s took place over five weeks in Washington, D.C. In an unprecedented act of Congress, Billy was allowed to conduct a service on the Capitol steps. The February day dawned cold and rainy, but thousands stood in the rain to hear the now famous evangelist. The sergeant-at-arms estimated the crowd to be larger than at most presidential inaugurations.

"I think the one that suffered perhaps the most, and without even knowing it, was Bill because he missed all those happy times when they were growing up and all the interesting things the children said and did and just being with them." ~ *Ruth Graham*

YOUNG FAMILY

Billy's popularity spread like wildfire. Here was a handsome, articulate, sincere, down-to-earth man who preached the unadulterated Word of God—and lived it, too. He caught the nation's fancy, and so did the message he brought. *The Hour of Decision* steadily gained listeners each week, and letters poured into the tiny office in Minneapolis, many seeking advice for personal problems.

Of course, the more famous Billy and his ministry became, the more he needed to travel. "The biggest event for the children," Ruth said, "was when Daddy was home. They were mighty good about him being gone so much because they knew why he was gone."

When it was time for the inevitable good-bye, neither Ruth nor Billy displayed emotion. There was the tight hug and kiss. But in private, they were quite different. "Many a time," Billy said, "I've driven down that driveway with tears coming down my cheeks, not wanting to leave."

OPPOSITE: *The sight of Billy saying good-bye to Ruth and Bunny was a familiar, if painful, one.*

ABOVE: *William Franklin Graham III was born July 14, 1952. Billy said, "I would have loved another girl, but every man needs a son."*

ABOVE RIGHT: *Gigi, Anne, Bunny, Ruth, and Billy relaxed with the family dog in Montreat.*

RIGHT: *Anne, Gigi, Franklin, and Bunny shared a bedtime story with their mother.*

INQUISITIVE VISITORS AT HOME

Determined to see where the Grahams called home, curiosity seekers descended on the small hamlet of Montreat, tucked into a picturesque valley in the Blue Ridge Mountains. They poked around the main roads and paraded up and down neat residential lanes. They trampled through Ruth's flowerbeds and peered into the windows . . . at all hours. They meant no harm, but their presence was disturbing, sometimes upsetting.

Ruth worked out her own classification for the "friendly intruders." If they barreled right into the yard, they were usually from the Baptist campground at nearby Ridgecrest. If they simply stopped for a quick look, they were most likely Southern Presbyterian. Only the Episcopalians drove past at a discreet pace.

Determined not to let the family become public property, the Grahams kept the children away from the public—especially the press—and refused to put them on display at crusades. They were normal kids.

TOP: *Billy's study had a large window and was level with the road. He was sometimes forced to crawl on all fours from his desk to the door to escape the eyes of curious tourists.*

ABOVE: *A sign made by Billy's children warned visitors about the family's three dogs.*

OPPOSITE: *Anne, Ruth, Bunny, Gigi, Franklin, and Billy enjoyed a fall day together.*

"One day I noticed that Bunny had more spending money than her allowance would afford and I asked where it came from. Gigi said, 'Why don't you watch her?' So I did, and the next time a tour bus pulled up, all Bunny had to do was walk up to that busload of tourists with her little friendly face. She didn't ask for money, but the purse was quite obvious. I watched those people just automatically dropping dimes and quarters in her bag while they asked her questions. We put a stop to that in no time flat!" ∽ *Ruth Graham*

"Bill and I settled on a new house site about a mile straight up the mountain as a crow flies from Montreat. We paid $12.50 to $14.00 an acre for the land. The surveyors had difficulty because of the rambunctious terrain but finally agreed to call it two hundred acres." ～ *Ruth Graham*

A NEW HOME IN THE MOUNTAINS

In 1954 the Grahams purchased two hundred acres of mountaintop land on which they could build a new home, away from the main roads and so inaccessible that at last the problem of peeking tourists would be solved.

Two years later, the Grahams started building, and Ruth began to design. She scoured the mountains, buying old timber from abandoned log cabins and bricks from an old schoolhouse. With its split-rail fences, the outside of the home looked as if it were a century old. Inside, it had a classic, informal country-house atmosphere.

Six days before the start of his New York crusade in 1957, Billy made this entry in his personal diary: "This is the first spring that I have ever spent at home. What a wonderful and thrilling few weeks this has been: to run and play with my children every day, to listen to their problems. Today, Ruth and I took our last stroll. What a wonderful companion she is. Little Franklin keeps pleading, 'Daddy don't go!' I have come to love this mountaintop and would like nothing better than for the Lord to say I should stay here for the rest of my life."

OPPOSITE: *Billy and Ruth enjoyed a picnic near the site of their new home.*

ABOVE: *The family's new home was built on a mountaintop.*

"Our large property in Montreat offered us some much-needed privacy, and it gave Ruth and me the ability to connect with our children. Many times I would take our children to a special spot on top of the mountain for some time alone. We would sit on a log or a rock and just talk."

～ *Billy Graham*

LONDON: THE MINISTRY REACHES ABROAD

Billy was facing the greatest test of his young ministry. The Greater London Crusade was scheduled for three months: March through May 1954. Billy, whose ministry was not yet well established outside the United States, was tense. He insisted that Ruth accompany him—he needed her support. Ruth was uneasy, but she joined Billy in England. It was her longest separation from the children.

As with the Los Angeles campaign, the press helped establish Billy Graham's name in London—but this time, the results were markedly different. "It all started," Billy said, "when our Minneapolis office printed a calendar telling about our London crusade. One word mysteriously got changed, which brought on me the wrath of the Labour party and the British press. After discovering what I allegedly had said, I could not blame them. The statement was, 'What Hitler's bombs could not do, socialism' (which had been substituted for my word secularism) 'with its accompanying evils, shortly accomplished.' The mistake was discovered and corrected before many had been printed but somehow one of the uncorrected copies got to London and into the hands of one newspaperman and a member of Parliament."

The press was harsh at first, but gradually, after interviews and press conferences, some reporters grudgingly acknowledged the American evangelist's skill and patience in answering their tricky and antagonistic questions.

TOP: *Despite their chilly reception from the press, the Grahams were nearly lost in the waiting crowd at Waterloo Station.*

ABOVE: *Billy and Archbishop of Canterbury Geoffrey Fisher chatted on their way to the platform at Wembley Stadium.*

OPPOSITE: *Just before they came out on deck, Billy asked Ruth not to wear any lipstick because some British clergy rated lipstick worldly and Billy wanted to please them. She refused. Ruth wrote in her diary: "Bill stooped from being a man of God to become a meddlesome husband, so I said it doesn't seem to me to be a credit to Christ to be drab. I think it is a Christian's duty to look as nice as possible. Besides, not caring about one's appearance goes against a woman's nature. That's not going to make anybody a better Christian, either. And it's not fair to the people who have to look at you. I believe my lipstick did help."*

"The day before the crusade was to open, the *People* newspaper hurled abuse at 'Silly Billy.' Grady even heard a reporter grandly announce, 'When Jesus was on earth, He rode a lowly donkey. I cannot imagine Jesus arriving in England on a great ocean liner!' Grady fired back, 'Listen, man, if you can find me a donkey that can swim the Atlantic, I'll buy it on the spot.'" ~ *Billy Graham*

THE LONDON CRUSADE

The London crusade remains one of the high spots in Billy's career. From March 1 until May 22, he held nightly meetings in North London's Harringay Arena. The stakes were high: no speaker had ever filled the twelve-thousand-seat arena for more than one night. And the cost was unprecedented—thirty-three thousand pounds, about one hundred thousand dollars!

That first evening was, in some ways, the most memorable of Billy's ministry. The meeting was set for 7:00 p.m. But the weather was foul, even drearier than usual. Just as Ruth and Billy were leaving for the eight-mile drive to the arena, they received a message that there were just two thousand people in their seats—only a handful in that big place. Meanwhile, more than three hundred press and camera people were watching and waiting.

"Ruth and I held hands in silence as we drove through the wet streets," Billy recalled. "I thought of the gloating stories that they would write and I thought of the thousands of prayers from around the world for that night. We just tried to prepare our hearts to face whatever God had planned. When we arrived and walked into Harringay, I could hardly believe my eyes. It seemed that thousands had poured out of the Underground to fill the arena while Ruth and I were en route those long eight miles from the hotel. Tears of gratefulness to God welled up."

In the end, Billy reached more people than he ever thought possible. The arena overflowed with eager attendees. The crusade was so popular, in fact, that the team had to create "landline relays" (live broadcasts by telephone lines) that carried the services to more than four hundred halls and churches all across the British Isles.

TOP AND ABOVE: *Billy preached before record numbers in Harringay Arena, 1954.*

OPPOSITE: *From the beginning, the London crusade was very popular, and it remained so throughout the entire three months.*

"I learned more about human nature in two hours at Harringay than I have learned in thirty-seven years. I realized the power for good . . . or for evil that can be released. Of the longing of people for a different sort of life. Of course, if I wanted to be clever I would just say man needs a God. . . . But you see that wouldn't really express what I was feeling. For all the way home I puffed at my pipe. My eyes were scalded with tears."

∽ *William Hickey,* London Daily Express

"At the end of the first week our arena was jammed an hour before meeting time, and the police reported that thirty thousand had failed to get in. By the end of the first month, Londoners were almost fighting for free tickets. Socialites came to see and to hear and to be converted. Bishops were willing to sit with us on the platform. Even newspapers became friendly." ∽ *Billy Graham*

TRAFALGAR SQUARE AND HYDE PARK

The meetings at Harringay were so popular that the team soon began holding outdoor rallies. One Saturday afternoon, April 3, 1954, Trafalgar Square was packed as it had not been since VE Day. A few weeks later, on a warm, sunny Good Friday, the team held an open-air rally in Hyde Park. The crowds—estimated by London police to be more than fifty thousand people—covered half a square mile. The message was fitting: "God forbid that I should glory, save in the cross of our Lord Jesus Christ."

The final meetings were scheduled in the two largest stadiums in London: Wembley and White City, with both meetings the same afternoon. On that last day, Billy preached to about two hundred thousand people, the largest religious gathering in British history. Over a period of three months, more than two million British subjects had heard Billy preach, and more than thirty-eight thousand had made decisions for Christ.

ABOVE: *The crowd listened raptly as Billy preached in Trafalgar Square.*

BELOW LEFT: *By the end of the first month in Britain, the newspapers had become friendly and were giving Billy's crusades all-out support.*

SIR WINSTON CHURCHILL

On Billy's scheduled day of departure, he was summoned on short notice to No. 10 Downing Street by Prime Minister Sir Winston Churchill, who had carried Britain through World War II and was already listed in history as one of the greatest statesmen of all time.

Sir Winston asked Billy, "Do you have any hope? What hope do you have for the world?" Billy took out his little New Testament and answered, "Mr. Prime Minister, I am filled with hope."

Sir Winston pointed at the early editions of three London evening papers lying on the table. They were filled with reports of rape, murder, and hate. When he was a boy it was different, he told Billy. "I am an old man," he said, "and without hope for the world."

Billy replied, "Life is very exciting because I know what is going to happen in the future." He paged through the New Testament and explained the meaning of Christ's birth, His death, and His resurrection. He then went on to speak of the Second Coming of Christ. The brief time that had been scheduled for their meeting was extended to forty minutes. At last Sir Winston said, "I do not see much hope for the future unless it is the hope you are talking about, young man. We must have a return to God."

TOP: *As Billy left his meeting with Sir Winston Churchill, he said to the press, "I feel like I have shaken hands with history."*

ABOVE: *At the end of Billy's time with Churchill, he prayed for the prime minister, asking God's help for the many difficult situations Mr. Churchill faced each day.*

"My phone rang, and a voice at the other end said that Sir Winston Churchill wanted me for lunch the following day. I was so tired, I replied, 'It's impossible. We're taking a train tonight.' Aghast, I realized that I had turned down the prime minister of Great Britain. Within minutes, the phone rang again, and the voice asked, 'Could you come today at twelve?' I dressed and shot over." ∼ *Billy Graham*

QUEEN ELIZABETH II

The following year, the team moved the crusades to Scotland, and on Easter Sunday, Billy was accorded the privilege of preaching to the Queen and the Duke of Edinburgh in their private chapel at the Royal Lodge.

"A note from Buckingham Palace was handed to me privately during our crusade in Glasgow, Scotland, in 1955," Billy vividly recalled. "It invited me to preach at Windsor Castle and asked Ruth and me to lunch afterward with Her Majesty Queen Elizabeth and Prince Philip."

The visit left a lasting impression. "Good manners do not permit one to discuss the details of a private visit with Her Majesty," Billy recollected, "but I can say that I judge her to be a woman of rare modesty and character. I made a pledge to remember the Queen and her family every day in my prayers."

"When we filed into the Royal Chapel, I was stunned to realize that it had no pulpit, just a place to stand. I carried a thick sheaf of handwritten notes on extra paper and was forced to leave them behind when I got up to speak. I had prayed so much about this moment that I knew however simple and full of mistakes my sermon would be, God would overrule and use it—but I'll tell you, I could really feel my heart beating!" ∽ *Billy Graham*

OPPOSITE: *Billy and Ruth were dressed for one of several formal occasions in Britain.*

ABOVE: *At the Queen's request, Billy visited Windsor Castle.*

ABOVE RIGHT AND RIGHT: *Queen Elizabeth and Prince Philip invited Billy to preach in their private chapel at the Royal Lodge.*

THE QUEEN HEARS BILLY GRAHAM

COURT CIRCULAR. WINDSOR CASTLE. 22ND MAY, 1955.
THE QUEEN AND THE DUKE OF EDINBURGH ATTENDED DIVINE SERVICE THIS MORNING IN THE PRIVATE CHAPEL, THE ROYAL LODGE. DR. WILLIAM GRAHAM PREACHED THE SERMON.

The Queen hears Billy Graham

He preaches the sermon in Royal Lodge chapel

Western Mail

MADISON SQUARE GARDEN
—By Mike Parks

WEDNESDAY, JUNE 5, 1957

BILLY GRAHAM

"I always face the press and television with fear, anxiety, and complete dependence on the Lord. I think I pray as much about a press conference as I do about my sermons. It is so easy to be misquoted and misinterpreted. I have never believed that the success of our work depends on, or is the result of, publicity. However, I am convinced that God has used the press and TV coverage in our work, and it has been one of the most effective factors in sustaining public interest through the years."

~ *Billy Graham*

"For two years in the mid-fifties, more newspaper and magazine copy was devoted to Billy Graham than to any other person in the United States, including President Eisenhower." ~ *William Martin,* Texas Monthly

"My challenge to the press of America would be, let's work for the reversal of the runaway trend toward moral degeneracy that has destroyed so many nations in the past. Let's seek an emphasis on positive virtues. And let's communicate the fact that fundamental moral values have the same power to heal the minds, hearts, and souls of people as they've always had."

~ *Billy Graham, addressing the National Press Club*

"Everything he does is compelling. He is made of the stuff that molds men's minds, stuff that has destroyed nations when activated by a Hitler or a Mussolini, that has saved nations when embodied in an Abraham Lincoln or a Winston Churchill."

~ *Dwight Newton, San Francisco journalist*

"ABOUT YOUR SERMON, MR. PRESIDENT"

ONLY NUDIST CAN TOP BILLY—

Evangelist Graham Meets Ike And Nixon Clad Only in Towel

INDIANAPOLIS — (UP) — Evangelist Billy Graham Wednesday staked claim to a curious clerical "first" that's not likely to be topped very soon.

Graham thinks he's the only minister ever to conduct an audience with the president and vice president of the United States while splendidly, if not decorously, clad in a bath towel.

"It happened last Monday at Burning Tree Country club in Washington," Graham said,

grinning as he told of the incident in an impromptu hotel room news conference.

"Mr. Nixon and I had just finished a round of golf, and I was taking a shower. The vice president came in and said Mr. Eisenhower had just entered the clubhouse after playing, and he wanted to talk to me.

"I just grabbed a towel and came out—guess I didn't think anything about it being unusual. Later Mr. Nixon told me that I probably was the first minister ever to talk with the president and vice president under just those conditions."

"Bishop . . . The repair man is here . . . !"

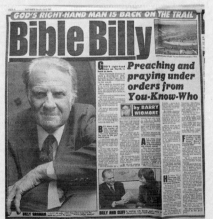

"In this day of publicity and media exposure, people have a tendency to feel that you are larger than life. Many people put me on a pedestal where I do not belong. I am not the holy, righteous prophet of God that many people think I am. I share with Wesley [John Wesley, an eighteenth-century English evangelist] the feeling of my own inadequacy and sinfulness constantly. I am often amazed that God can use me at all."

≈ *Billy Graham*

Those who wanted to hear the Word of God weren't the only ones interested in Billy— the press followed his every move as well. These are just a few of the many cartoons and newspaper articles that illustrate the effect Billy had on popular culture.

At first, Billy was overwhelmed by the size of New York City and the needs of its people, but he quickly found God at work there. Almost one hundred thousand people made decisions for Christ as a result of Billy's four-month-long New York crusade—a milestone for the new ministry.

LEFT: *Crowds lined up early to see Billy at Madison Square Garden.*

ABOVE: *En route to New York by train, Billy made a brief stop in Washington to visit his old friend President Eisenhower.*

THE NEW YORK MILESTONE

In 1957, New York presented as great a challenge to Billy Graham as London had. But with typical thoroughness, the team prepared 40,000 bumper stickers, 250,000 crusade songbooks, 100,000 Gospels of John, 1,000,000 fliers, 35,000 window posters, and 650 billboards posted at strategic locations within the city.

The crusade was scheduled for six weeks at Madison Square Garden, and as in London, it was a success, with record-breaking numbers of people in attendance. At the end of the crusade, a historic meeting was held in Yankee Stadium. More than 100,000 gathered inside while thousands of others pushed at the gates, trying to gain entrance. After the Yankee Stadium rally, the crusade was extended to September 1—and the final rally was held in Times Square.

The crusade finally came to a close after sixteen weeks. During that time, more than 2.3 million people heard the Word of God, 60,000 made decisions for Christ, and another 30,000 professed by mail the decisions they had made while watching live telecasts.

"I believe the Lord would have us go to hard places. Over half the people in this great metropolis of New York are completely unchurched. However, I am convinced that in the sight of God and by heaven's evaluation this crusade will be no failure and Christ will receive the glory and honor. I have prayed, worried, and wept over New York more than any other place in which we have held a crusade." ∽ *Billy Graham*

The New York crusade was supported by 1,500 churches, which supplied volunteer workers to help each night.

Historic Yankee Stadium was filled to overflowing on the hottest day of the year—105 degrees in the shade.

YANKEE STADIUM

The Yankee Stadium rally on July 20, 1957, was meant to be the climax of the New York crusade. More than one hundred thousand people attended—including some famous faces. When Billy made his entrance, walking beside him across the field was Richard Nixon.

"I bring you a message from one who is a very good friend of Billy Graham's," Vice President Nixon told the crowd, "and one who would have been here if his duties had allowed him—the greetings and best wishes of President Eisenhower."

At the close of his message, because there was not room, Billy could not ask inquirers to come forward to the platform. Instead, he asked all who would acknowledge Christ as their Savior to stand—and literally thousands rose from their seats.

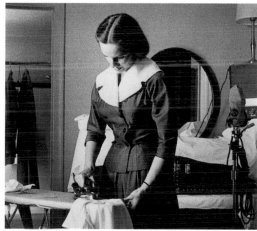

"I have lived in New York City for twenty-five years, and through my church and interdenominational contacts have had the opportunity to appraise the spiritual life of the city for a quarter of a century. I would like to testify that never in this period of time has there been anything even remotely approximating the profound spiritual impact which Billy Graham has made on New York City. For the first time there has been a definite soul-searching on the part of the people. . . . I have never seen prayer take hold as it did in the days preceding the crusade, and as it continued all the way through." ∾ *Ruth Peale (Mrs. Norman Vincent Peale)*

TOP LEFT: *Billy saw the New York media as a welcome opportunity to spread the Gospel.*

TOP: *Vice President Richard Nixon joined the audience in prayer on the platform during the Yankee Stadium rally.*

ABOVE: *Retreating from a round of newspaper interviews, Ruth ironed her husband's shirts. Broadcast equipment for* **The Hour of Decision** *filled the corner of their hotel room.*

"We have not come to put on a show or an entertainment. We believe that there are many people here tonight that have hungry hearts—all your life, you've been searching for peace, joy, happiness, and forgiveness. I want to tell you that you can find everything that you have been searching for in Christ." ∞ *Billy Graham*

TELECASTS BEGIN

At the height of the New York campaign, the American Broadcasting Company made a prime-time hour available each Saturday night. To pay for the initial contract of four weekly telecasts, the evangelist received from a foundation the largest single gift that had ever been made to his association—one hundred thousand dollars.

The impact was tremendous. Suddenly, Billy was preaching into the nation's living rooms. In the end, seventeen telecasts were made from Madison Square Garden to an estimated seven million viewers each week, the largest single congregation to hear the Gospel up to that time.

By the late 1950s, most Americans had heard of Billy Graham, but only a fraction had ever experienced a crusade. Now, viewers could watch from the comfort of their living rooms to see what Billy Graham was really all about. "We are reaching more through these telecasts," Billy marveled, "than we could reach in a lifetime in Madison Square Garden."

ABOVE LEFT: *An estimated ninety-six million people viewed one or more of the seventeen live Saturday telecasts in 1957. Viewers sent in more than 1.5 million letters during the telecast.*

ABOVE: *Billy's powerful preaching drew crowds to Madison Square Garden and prompted favorable media coverage.*

OPPOSITE: *On July 10, 1957, a lunch-hour meeting occurred in lower Manhattan, where secretaries, clerks, and financiers stood shoulder to shoulder to hear the Gospel.*

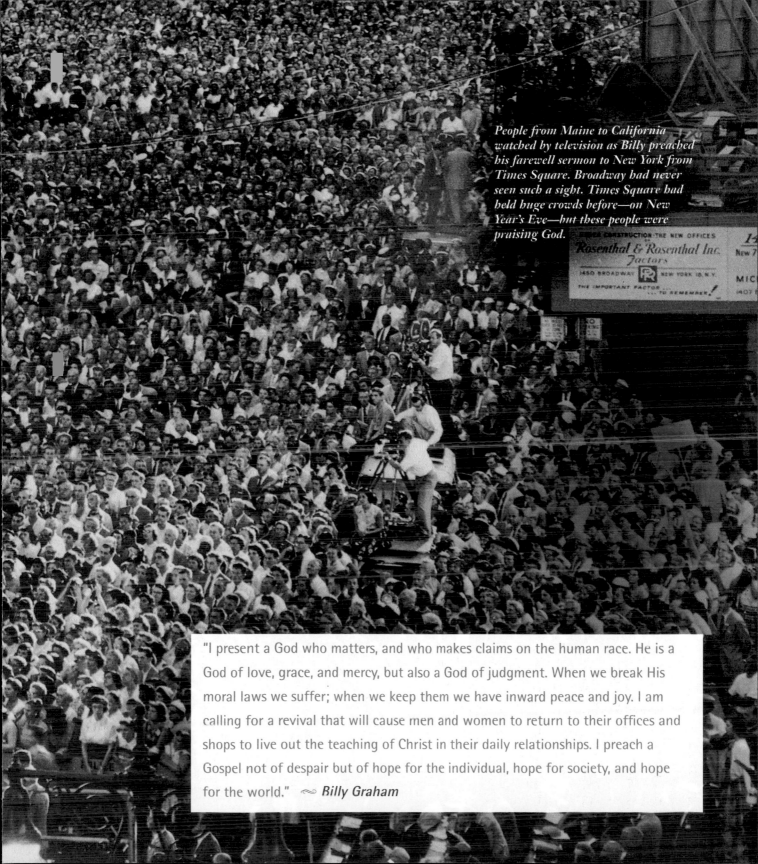

People from Maine to California watched by television as Billy preached his farewell sermon to New York from Times Square. Broadway had never seen such a sight. Times Square had held huge crowds before—on New Year's Eve—but these people were praising God.

"I present a God who matters, and who makes claims on the human race. He is a God of love, grace, and mercy, but also a God of judgment. When we break His moral laws we suffer; when we keep them we have inward peace and joy. I am calling for a revival that will cause men and women to return to their offices and shops to live out the teaching of Christ in their daily relationships. I preach a Gospel not of despair but of hope for the individual, hope for society, and hope for the world." ∾ *Billy Graham*

Chapter Three

Millions of Lives Changed

Billy Graham preached the Gospel face-to-face to more than one hundred million people on six continents, in eighty-four countries, and in all of America's fifty states. His crusades across the globe—in Europe, Asia, North and South America, Australia, and Africa—broke stadium attendance records. And with the advent of radio, television, and satellite broadcasts, Billy was able to reach more than two billion people.

News of his first crusades in Los Angeles, London, and New York traveled like lightning around the world. As invitations to hold crusades began pouring in from every continent, Billy and his team evaluated each opportunity, formulating a decision-making procedure that Franklin Graham and the BGEA continue to this day. Before accepting any invitation, the ministry considers criteria ranging from community needs, local interest, and available meeting facilities, to time and even weather conditions.

One of the most important considerations has always been local church support. Early on, Billy and his team decided to accept only those invitations that came from unified groups of ministers and laypeople from many different churches who wanted to spread the Gospel to their community. But ultimately, Billy always made the final decision himself, after much prayer.

A BGEA crusade leaves an unmistakable imprint on its host city, whether it

OPPOSITE: *On September 22, 1991, more than 250,000 people attended New York's Central Park rally, making it the largest North American crusade event ever.*

BELOW: *Billy was eager to spread the Good News to the people of Asia, a culture that he found to be "richly diverse."*

"Billy Graham is truly a man sent by God to deliver the message of Jesus Christ. I have met countless people in Pittsburgh and all over the country who really had their lives changed—or at least the seeds were planted—at a Billy Graham crusade. I don't think we will ever know how many leaders in this county, both religious and otherwise, have been impacted by a Billy Graham crusade. And many times it isn't felt for ten to twenty years." ❧ *C. Fred Fetterolf, former president and COO of Alcoa, and chairman of the 1993 Pittsburgh crusade*

is domestic or overseas. If only for a brief time, people become aware of God through the advertising and publicity that takes place. Suddenly, Christians grow less afraid to talk to their friends and neighbors about their belief in God. People who come forward at a crusade are given Bible study materials and referred back to their local churches, which receive many new members anxious to know God. Then as individual lives are changed, these changes touch families, families touch communities, and communities touch cities—and then countries—longing for renewal.

Businesses typically measure a meeting's success in terms of attendance and response statistics. Billy, however, had a different standard for his crusades. "If I talk to one person and get him to say yes to Jesus Christ," he often said, "I consider that to be a successful meeting."

ABOVE: *Torrential rain did not dampen the response to the Gospel message at London's Wembley Stadium in 1989.*

OPPOSITE: *Over three hundred thousand people attended the Greater Los Angeles Billy Graham crusade over three nights at the Rose Bowl in 2005.*

"The real story of the crusades is not in the great choirs, the thousands in attendance, nor the hundreds of inquirers who are counseled. The real story is in the changes that have taken place in the hearts and lives of people."

～ *Billy Graham*

ABOVE: *A counselor used sign language to communicate with a blind and deaf inquirer.*

OPPOSITE: *Billy talked to the thousands who came forward to ask Jesus Christ into their lives at the Greater New York crusade in 2005.*

"There are four things that are very important to help you as a new believer: first, read the Bible. It is God's Word, written to you. Second, pray. Take everything to God in prayer, because He loves you and you are now His child. Talk to God like you would your best friend. Third, witness for Christ. Tell someone about your decision for Christ. Then witness by your smile and by your love and concern for others. Fourth, get into a church where Christ is proclaimed and where you can serve Him." ∾ *Billy Graham*

"I used to think Jesus was for the birds. To be frank, I hated Him. I had tried everything, including Buddhism and an Indian guru, vegetarianism and LSD, political rallies and marches, rock concerts and grass. Then one evening I flipped on the TV and your crusade was being telecast. Then I knew what I had been searching for. That night Jesus came to live in me. He filled me with happiness and peace. He surrounded me with love. He took away my tears." ∾ *A new Christian from Phoenix, Arizona*

CHANGED LIVES: THE OBJECTIVE

All ages, all nationalities, all races, all religions, both rich and poor, educated and uneducated—thousands of people from all walks of life have testified to the way Christ changed their lives after they came forward at a Billy Graham crusade.

Billy always issued the invitation with these words: "I'm going to ask hundreds of you to get up out of your seats and come and stand here and say by coming, 'I am willing to acknowledge that I have sinned—I have broken God's laws. I am ready to change my way of living, and receive Christ and follow Him, no matter what the cost.' I am asking you to make that commitment right now. You can say yes to Christ, and a great transformation can take place inside of you. You can become a new person. You may be Catholic, Protestant, Jewish; you may not have any religion, but God is speaking to you and you know you need Christ.

"All I am is a messenger to tell you that God loves you, Christ died for you, and He will forgive you when you receive Him into your heart. You are not coming to me; you are coming to Christ. I have no supernatural power; I cannot save you.

"The night that I came to Christ, the evangelist extended the invitation for quite a long time. And I was the last to come. And I'm glad that he waited. If God is speaking to you, this is your moment with God—you come."

"I'm going to ask you to bow your heads, and I want you to pray this prayer after me. Pray it out loud. 'Oh God, I am a sinner. I am sorry for my sins. I am willing to turn from my sins. I receive Christ as my Savior. I confess Him as Lord. From this moment on, I want to follow Him and serve Him in the fellowship of His church. In Christ's name, Amen.'"

~ Billy Graham

CLOCKWISE FROM FAR LEFT: *A volunteer helped a fellow countryman make a decision for Christ in Scotland in 1991; a volunteer prayed with a young girl who responded to Billy's message; volunteers sometimes use pamphlets to help communicate the Gospel message; thousands turned out to hear Billy preach in Madras, India, 1977; each crusade comes equipped to assist the elderly or disabled.*

"There are so many gods in Japan. I was at a loss as to how to get to heaven. This is the first time that I learned I get to heaven through Jesus Christ." ∾ *A crusade attendee from Tokyo*

"They've come to make life's most important commitment. I feel terribly unworthy at that moment. I feel terribly inadequate to help them. I know it has to be of God, that I can't do anything. No matter what they do for the rest of their lives, for one moment they've stood before God." ∾ *Billy Graham*

"For five years I was in a private hell. I was on two different anti-depressants and two different tranquilizers. During the Las Vegas crusade telecast I accepted Jesus as my personal Savior. Many times I had wished I could start all over again, and now I have."

~ *A crusade attendee from Providence,* Rhode Island

"I joined in to try and find out just what special magic it is that keeps the crowds pouring in. There was no Bible thumping or fanatical evangelism to drive people wild. Just a senior-looking man in a crisp blue suit saying his piece for those who wanted to hear." ~ *A British reporter*

CLOCKWISE FROM TOP LEFT: *Music has always been an essential part of each crusade, no matter what country it is held in; volunteers pray with everyone who comes forward at a crusade; at Billy's insistence, his earliest crusades were always integrated; a crusade volunteer prayed with an attendee after the message; people from many walks of life came to hear Billy preach.*

"People do not come to hear what I have to say—they want to know what God has to say." ∼ *Billy Graham*

The 1996 Charlotte crusade in Billy's hometown attracted over seventy-five thousand people on its closing night.

ABOVE: *In March 1973 Johannesburg's Wanderers Stadium held sixty thousand people, making it the largest multiracial gathering ever held in South Africa to that time.*

"I am convinced, through my travels and experiences, that people all over the world are hungry to hear the Word of God. As the people came to a desert place to hear John the Baptist proclaim, 'Thus saith the Lord,' so modern man in his confusions, frustrations, and bewilderment will come to hear the minister who preaches with authority." ∾ *Billy Graham*

CRUSADES AROUND THE WORLD

From his first crusade in London in the 1950s, Billy made preaching overseas an important part of his ministry. Traveling to Asia, Africa, North and South America, Europe, Australia, and New Zealand, he transformed the lives of individuals and in doing so, made historic inroads into many countries.

In January 1960 Billy made his first trip to Africa, preaching for three months across the continent. He traveled more than fourteen thousand miles, speaking to capacity crowds in large stadiums and small groups out in the bush. *Life* magazine covered part of his trip and reported on these landmark crusades, saying, "Billy talked to a third of a million Africans. . . . Some of Africa's enthusiasm and Graham's accomplishments stemmed from his insistence on non-segregated meetings." In fact, Billy deliberately bypassed the Union of South Africa because of its apartheid policy of total segregation. He did not return until thirteen years later, when the government allowed integrated meetings in both Johannesburg and Durban.

In the 1970s and 1980s Billy made history again, traveling into what at the time were Communist-controlled countries. It was a part of the world where atheism was officially sanctioned, and tens of thousands of people, hungry for spiritual truth, gathered to hear Billy preach the Gospel. After the fall of Communism in the Soviet Union in 1992, he conducted his first full-scale religious crusade in Russia.

All around the world, people flocked to hear his message. In fact, the largest meeting Billy ever held was in Seoul, South Korea. There, 1.1 million people sat on an old, unused airplane runway and listened to him speak through thousands of loudspeakers that stretched for almost a mile.

Billy did not preach in foreign countries because he wanted to see the world—he went because God sent him. "I believe that God has sent us here at this particular time," he would often say. "I believe that He has work for us to do here. I believe there are people who are going to be reached in this crusade that could not be reached for Christ and the church in any other way, or at any other time."

"God is a God of love, a God of mercy. He has the hairs of your head numbered. . . . He wants to come into your life and give you new hope."

~ *Billy Graham*

BELOW: *River Plate Stadium in Buenos Aires, Argentina, in 1991*

BOTTOM RIGHT: *A trained counselor explained God's Word to local schoolchildren.*

BOTTOM LEFT: *A man listened intently to Billy's message.*

The Sydney Morning Herald,
May 4, 1979

BEHIND THE 'MAGIC' OF BILLY GRAHAM

Sir, Your paper's report on Monday night's Billy Graham crusade meeting referred to the crowds response to "the old Billy Graham mysterious magic."
There is no magic. What your reporter saw, and possibly did not understand was God at work. God could evoke the same response without Billy Graham but He choses instead to work through people. Billy Graham is just one of those people.
— K. A. Wilson

LEFT: *A large TV screen in the parking lot was provided for the overflow crowd at the Meadowlands Sports Complex in East Rutherford, New Jersey.*

BELOW LEFT: *Billy preached to a record crowd of 55,300 at Mile High Stadium in Denver, Colorado, in 1987.*

"I'm grateful to Dr. Graham and his organization for bringing the Gospel of Jesus Christ to Columbus and to Ohio. With the breakdown of religious, moral, and family values, Dr. Graham's evangelism is needed more today than ever before in our nation's history. Thank you, Dr. Graham, for spending one week in your life with us so that one day we will be able to share eternal life with our Father in heaven. Your witness and words have brought about a spiritual awakening—a new beginning for the 150,000 central Ohio souls who have attended this crusade." ~ *George Voinovich, former governor of Ohio*

"In 1984 I was getting ready to go out at night and party. My TV was turned on, and a Billy Graham crusade was on. For an hour I sat down and watched this program. This was the man my mom and dad watched when I was a kid. There I sat on my bed, dressed up and ready to go out and party, and there came Billy Graham speaking God's Word. He wasn't making it easy. The Word of God pierced my heart, convinced me of my sin, and at the end of the program, I called that phone number on the screen. A lady talked and prayed for me—like she knew me. And that changed my life. She prayed that I would have favor with God and man. And after that prayer my life changed and I started writing songs that were popular. I got rid of all the drugs and the alcohol. It proved to me that if we follow God's laws we will be the best we can be. That's what God did for me. I was living way below the level God wanted for me and I was missing out on all of His blessings."

~*Paul Overstreet*, *country-western songwriter*

ABOVE: *Temperatures on the platform registered 106 degrees at the Cincinnati crusade in 1972.*

LEFT: *Two boys read from* **My Decision**, *a book handed out after the message to inquirers.*

"Because of Billy Graham's visit, a new generation of leadership will emerge which will have a significant impact on the life of this city and even worldwide. My coming to Christ at the Billy Graham crusade in London in 1954 is a living example. I've given over twenty years of my life to the Christian ministry."

〜*Reverend John Guest*

ABOVE: *Thousands responded to Billy's invitation at the Georgia Dome in Atlanta, 1994.*

RIGHT: *One of the many crusade volunteers handed out programs to attendees.*

Operation Andrew
BILLY GRAHAM CRUSADE

"As one who has become a full-time volunteer in the crusade, I have been especially impressed with the high degree of professionalism in the Graham organization—even better than I found in the White House. Also, the ethical and spiritual integrity of the Graham team has served to further reinforce my previous opinion as to the character and reputation of Dr. Graham and his organization. All of this has increased the measure of my faith in our Lord and biblical Christianity." ∽ *Harry S. Dent, South Carolina crusade volunteer and former White House staff member*

VOLUNTEERS ARE THE KEY

Billy often said, "I am just one man among many that have come for this crusade. It's the Lord using my team of people along with the local churches to make Christ known to the community." Indeed, each BGEA crusade or festival is held with the assistance of thousands of volunteers who work, pray for, and help with the events in each city. Most of these events involve anywhere from five hundred to twelve hundred churches representing seventy to ninety different religious groups and beliefs. All told, local churches provide thousands of volunteers for a typical event.

Guided by a small number of staff members from the BGEA, a core group of fifty to one hundred volunteers fulfill a wide range of duties, completing tasks like forming committees, securing funding, and arranging for the facility. An additional ten thousand participate in prayer groups. Before the crusade or festival begins, these volunteers pray for the team and for the thousands of people who will attend and eventually come forward to make a commitment to Christ.

During the actual event, more than one thousand men and women fill the role of ushers, and typically five thousand serve as counselors. Meeting one-on-one, they talk and pray with every person who responds to the invitation to come forward. A three-hundred-person team keeps track of all those who came forward, so that each may be sent information about nearby churches. Finally, literally thousands of other volunteers serve as visitation workers, following up with a personal visit or telephone call to those who came forward at an event.

ABOVE LEFT: *Taking to heart the biblical story of Andrew who "went to find his brother . . . and he brought him to meet Jesus" (John 1:40–42), members of area churches are urged to reach out to their neighbors and bring them to crusade meetings.*

ABOVE: *A volunteer prayed with a young girl at one of Billy's international crusades.*

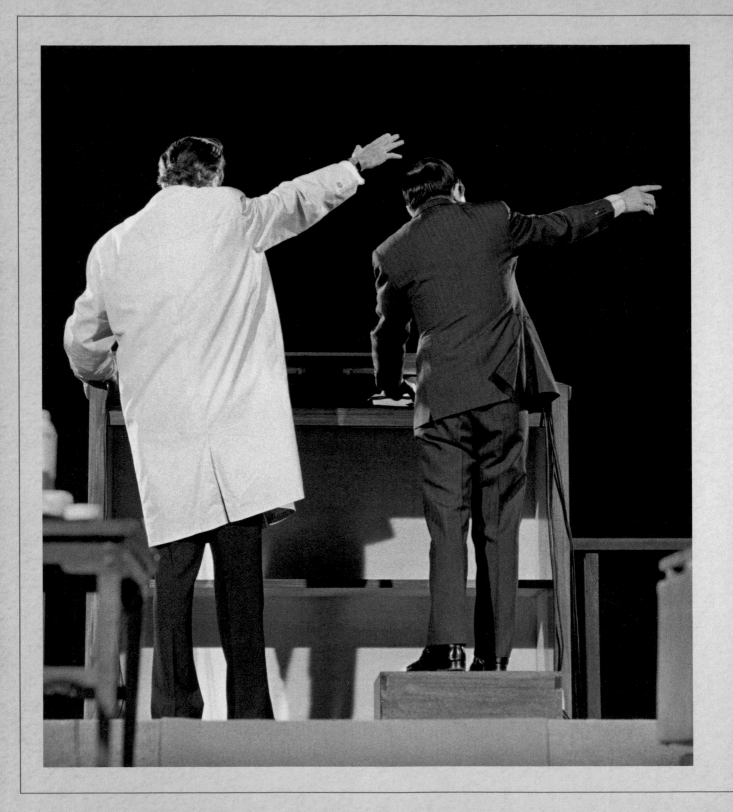

> "I am convinced the greatest act of love we can ever perform for people is to tell them about God's love for them in Christ."
>
> ~ *Billy Graham*

John 3:16...

— John 1:12 "But as many as received him, to them gave he power to become the sons of God, even to them that believe on his name."

— Romans 4:5 "To him that worketh not, but believeth on him that justifieth the ungodly, his faith is counted for righteousness."

— Ephesians 2:8: "For by grace are ye saved through faith."

ABOVE: *Billy visited Uhuru Park in Nairobi, Kenya, in 1976.*

LEFT: *An Australian volunteer reviewed the Gospel message with a young woman.*

ABOVE RIGHT: *When preaching, Billy referred to the Bible and to outline-style notes he prepared in advance.*

OPPOSITE: *In Seoul, South Korea, 1973, translator Billy Kim interpreted every word and gesture.*

ABOVE: *Stadium lights over Anfield in Liverpool, England, illuminated the 1984 crusade.*

FAR LEFT: *In 1984 Billy preached in a chilling wind and below-freezing temperatures in Sunderland, England, near the North Sea.*

LEFT: *Houston businessman and longtime BGEA board member Carloss Morris counseled a young, physically disabled inquirer.*

"For thirty-seven years my life was miserable. I went through two broken marriages and for many years suffered terrible depressions. . . . I didn't feel that life was worth living, and sometimes I wished that I were dead. . . . I saw a leaflet announcing that Billy Graham would be coming. . . . I knew nothing about him but decided that I would go to hear him. That night I asked Jesus Christ into my heart. I handed my whole life over to Him, and I can't begin to describe the wonderful peace, joy, and love that flowed into my life from that moment."

∽ *A crusade attendee from Blackpool, England*

TOP: *In 1960 Billy preached to one hundred thousand people at the Reichstag in West Berlin, Germany. One week after the meetings ended, access from East Berlin was stopped; less than a year later, the Berlin Wall was built.*

ABOVE LEFT: *Billy's 1987 Finland crusade was witnessed by 42,500 people at Helsinki's Olympic Stadium.*

ABOVE: *More than three thousand people filled Waldensian Church in Turin, Italy, in 1967.*

Preaching in Communist Lands

While thousands of people yearned to get out from behind Eastern Europe's Iron Curtain, Billy was looking for a way to get in. Since his first visit to Moscow in 1959, he had wanted to preach the Gospel in the Soviet Union. "I knew that the Soviet Christians had been praying for years for me to come and preach," said Billy, "but our visas did not permit public speaking in 1959."

In July 1967 Billy preached in Yugoslavia, conducting Eastern Europe's first open-air evangelistic meetings since World War II. Ten years later, with the help of Dr. Alexander Haraszti, a Hungarian-born surgeon, the first Hungarian meetings took place. It was not easy—it took Dr. Haraszti fifteen trips to Hungary to negotiate Billy's first visit—but after Billy's trip there, other Communist-bloc nations opened their doors to him as well.

The governments were cautious and often permitted no publicity or advertising. News of his coming was usually spread by word of mouth. Even Billy and his team were sometimes kept in the dark about meeting times, because officials believed every event might turn into an antigovernment demonstration. But Billy knew God was at work.

After Billy's return from Moscow, a New York reporter asked him, "Are you aware that the Soviet government has used you for their propaganda?"

"Yes, I am," Billy answered, "but my propaganda is more powerful. We are using them to preach the Gospel of Jesus Christ to their people."

TOP: *In 1985 in Arad, Romania, people crowded an apartment building next to a church to hear Billy's message broadcast by loudspeaker.*

ABOVE: *In 1982 Billy preached in Moscow's Russian Orthodox Cathedral of the Epiphany.*

OPPOSITE: *In 1985 a crowd estimated at 150,000 greeted Billy in the public square outside the Ortho-dox cathedral in Timisoara, Romania.*

"Billy Graham was saying, 'Spirituality is alive in the Marxist, Leninist, Stalinist states. . . . It's there and I know it's there.' Frankly, there were all those years when I thought he was wrong or that he didn't know what he was talking about, but it turns out he was right." ～ *Dan Rather, broadcast journalist*

"Bill had always said that his life was not his own. His name had been lifted from obscurity by God. As he prayed about this decision, I knew that it was a simple matter. Regardless of his advisors, if Bill believed that God wanted him to preach in Soviet Russia, he would go." ∽ *Ruth Graham*

AN INVITATION TO THE SOVIET UNION

In 1982 the Soviet Union asked Billy to address an international religious leadership conference on the perils of nuclear war. He agonized over the invitation. The Soviet government often orchestrated these so-called peace conferences for propaganda purposes, and Billy feared being used as one of their tools. Many opposed the trip, but after much prayer, Billy decided to go, basing his decision on I Corinthians 9, in which the Apostle Paul wrote that we are to become all things to all men so that we might win some to God.

The meeting went so well that two years later, Billy conducted a twelve-day preaching mission in Leningrad, Tallinn, Novosibirsk, and Moscow. There, he gave fifty addresses, preaching in churches and universities, and speaking to citizens' groups and government and church officials. "There were no restrictions on my message," Billy marveled, "which is the same message I have preached throughout my ministry."

OPPOSITE: *In 1984 Billy met with the Russian media following a sermon in Moscow.*

TOP RIGHT: *Five thousand heard Billy's message in 1982 at* *the Patriarchal Cathedral of the Epiphany in Moscow.*

RIGHT: *Dozens of Soviets captured Billy's message on tape recorders.*

LEFT: *In 1985 the Second Baptist Church in Oradea, Romania, removed most of the pews to squeeze four thousand standing people into the small L-shaped church.*

BELOW LEFT: *In 1967 more than 3,500 heard Billy speak at a rainy Roman Catholic soccer field outside Zagreb, Yugoslavia's second-largest city.*

BELOW: *In 1977, with Dr. Haraszti interpreting, Billy spoke to thirty thousand at the Tahi Baptist Youth Camp in Hungary.*

"Nowhere in Mark 16:15—'Go ye into all the world, and preach the Gospel to every creature'—nor in any similar Scripture did Christ command us to go only into the Western or capitalist world. Nowhere did He say to exclude the Communist world."

❧ *Billy Graham*

ABOVE: *In 1978 Saint Ann's church in Cracow, Poland, the church of Pope John Paul II, welcomed Billy.*

TOP RIGHT: *In East Germany Billy preached from Martin Luther's pulpit in 1982.*

MIDDLE RIGHT: *In 1982 crowds filled every available space in the Brethren church of Bratislava, Czechoslovakia.*

RIGHT: *This little child may have had the best view in the crowded church.*

"Russia offers some measure of church freedom. But freedom is relative. I don't have freedom in the United States to go into a public school to preach the Gospel, nor is a student free in a public school to pray, or a teacher free to read the Bible publicly to the students. At the same time, we have a great deal of freedom for which I am grateful." ~ *Billy Graham*

CLOCKWISE FROM TOP LEFT: *Crowds filled every available space to hear Billy preach in Moscow's Baptist church in 1982; Billy met with Ambassador Dobrynin and Don Kendall; toppled statues of Stalin and other leaders graphically illustrated the end of Communist rule; and in May 1982, Billy delivered a major address in Moscow at a peace conference titled "Religious Workers for Saving the Sacred Gift of Life from Nuclear Catastrophe."*

LEFT: *In 1984 crowds swarmed Billy as he left the Orthodox church in Novosibirsk.*

BOTTOM LEFT: *In 1992, on the final Sunday afternoon at Moscow's Olympic Stadium, fifty thousand were jammed inside the thirty-five-thousand-seat auditorium while twenty thousand more* watched on a large-screen television.

BELOW: *In Tallinn, Metropolitan Alexy II (right), who later became Patriarch of the Russian Orthodox Church, listened to Billy's message at the Orthodox Cathedral of Alexander Nevsky in 1984.*

"I have stood in the places where history was made. I have seen with my own eyes the part that men and women of faith have played in these earthshaking events, and I have heard with my own ears their cries for freedom." — *Billy Graham*

"You have made many friends and your visit will have much influence. We are grateful for your sincere messages."

~ *Zhang Wenjin, Chinese ambassador to the United States*

CHINA: NEW HORIZONS

In the late 1980s the Grahams were finally invited to visit China, and Ruth fulfilled a lifelong dream. "All our married life," Billy remembered, "Ruth had talked about China—and with good reason. China was where she was born and where she spent the first seventeen years of her life. Growing up in China gave Ruth a love for the Chinese people and their culture that has never left her."

During his April 1988 trip there, Billy visited five cities, preaching in churches and the university and meeting with scholars and students, political and government leaders. He, Ruth, and Franklin also traveled to Ruth's childhood home, driving through little villages with mud farmhouses, thatched roofs, water buffalo, and chickens.

Once there, Ruth showed Billy and Franklin her bedroom, an alcove under the eaves. "I spent a lot of time looking out the small window, reading my books and my Bible," said Ruth. "I loved it here."

Outside, a big surprise awaited her: several of her childhood friends had come to visit. "Most of the older Christians have gone on to heaven," one told her, "but the younger Christians are carrying on."

TOP: *Ruth showed Billy an alcove in the home where she grew up.*

MIDDLE: *Billy met with Premier Li Peng at the Pavilion of Lavender Light (China's White House).*

LEFT: *Childhood friends greeted Ruth in Huaiyin.*

NORTH KOREA

North Korea—the country that at one time had banned all religious activity and proclaimed itself "the first atheistic nation on earth"—was the last place Billy ever expected to visit. But in 1992, although North Korea was technically still at war with the U.S. (the conflict had ended in 1953, but only with a cease-fire, not a peace treaty), the Korean Christian Federation and the Korean Catholics Association invited Billy for a weeklong visit.

There, Billy addressed more than four hundred students at the prestigious Kim Il Sung University. He also preached in two new churches in Pyongyang, spoke to a gathering of pastors and seminary students, and met with many high-ranking officials, including President Kim Il Sung.

During his second trip there, in 1994, Billy gave interviews to several reporters on North Korean national television and spoke at the Great People's Study House (equivalent to America's Library of Congress). He also met with President Kim, delivering a verbal message from President Clinton, just as he had done for President Bush in 1992. President Kim embraced him. "I consider it a great honor," he said, "to have a friend like you in the United States."

TOP: *President Kim Il Sung greeted Billy in 1994.*

LEFT: *A towering statue of President Kim Il Sung in North Korea*

ABOVE: *Billy preached at the new Chilgol church during his 1994 visit. At left is Ned Graham, who accompanied his father on his trips to North Korea.*

"I am a member of the human race. I am a world citizen. I have a responsibility to my fellow humans, whatever their religion. And I am convinced that only Christ can meet the deepest needs of our world and our hearts. Christ alone can bring lasting peace—peace with God, peace among men and nations, and peace within our hearts. He transcends the political and social boundaries of our world." ~ *Billy Graham*

In July 1966 a capacity crowd of ninety-five thousand inside and eight thousand outside heard Billy at London's Wembley Stadium.

"I have had the privilege of preaching this Gospel on every continent in most of the countries of the world. And I have found that when I present the simple message of the Gospel of Jesus Christ, with authority, quoting the very Word of God—He takes that message and drives it supernaturally into the human heart." ~ *Billy Graham*

Chapter Four

Reaching Out to a Broken World

As a young Christian, Billy was clear about his responsibility to his immediate neighbor, and frequently spoke on the virtues of being a Good Samaritan. But not until he began to travel and see more of the world did he fully understand that the Gospel he preached carried with it a global responsibility linking all humanity. In reflecting on his early years he recalled, "I had no real idea that millions of people throughout the world lived on the knife-edge of starvation and that I personally had a responsibility toward them." Many years later, after witnessing the devastating aftermath of the San Francisco earthquake, he said, "We cannot, and we must not, isolate ourselves from the world in which we live and the problems it faces. . . . The Gospel of Christ has no meaning unless it's applied to our fellow man who hurts and is in need. That's our neighbor, and Jesus said we're to love our neighbor as ourselves."

Billy's status as a world figure, with access to heads of state and political leaders on every continent, enabled him to initiate a ministry of reconciliation. As part of his crusade structure, Billy encouraged the establishment of a Love-in-Action committee in each crusade city, with the specific responsibility of exploring ways to provide assistance to those in need in the local community. Through this ongoing effort, tons of food and clothing are provided to the homeless and others with special needs.

OPPOSITE: *When he visited the bombed-out homes of Belfast, Northern Ireland, in 1972, Billy witnessed firsthand the effects of human brutality.*

BELOW: *Billy relayed God's message of hope through his work with suffering people.*

"The spirit of reconciliation we today sense in many hearts of South Africans can be traced directly to the Billy Graham meetings held in Durban and Johannesburg in 1973. He was the one who demanded total integration for all of his meetings, and it was done. The Christians then realized that it can be done. From that moment on we were on the road to reconciliation." ∼ *Alpheus Zulu, in a September 1985 letter*

ABOVE: *Alpheus Zulu, bishop of Zululand, attended a crusade with Billy.*

RIGHT: *Billy's 1982 visit to Moscow provided an opportunity for him to speak out*

for the rights of people everywhere.

OPPOSITE: *The first fully integrated public meeting ever held in South Africa was the 1973 Billy Graham crusade in Durban.*

"As a Christian, I believe that we are all created in the image of God. I believe that God loves the whole world. . . . The life of no human being is cheap in the eyes of God, nor can it be in our own eyes." ∼ *Billy Graham*

SPEAKING OUT ON HUMAN RIGHTS

Billy's concern for racial equality extended beyond the U.S. In 1960, during a three-month tour of Africa, he deliberately avoided the Union of South Africa, where apartheid ruled. During Billy's tour, a group of South African clergymen urged him to come to their embattled country. He said he would do so only if multiracial meetings could be arranged. Although the clergymen said his terms could probably be met within two years, it was not until thirteen years later that the government permitted a desegregated crusade. In 1973 Billy held the first integrated public meetings in South Africa. There, he touched more than one hundred thousand people and thousands more via live radio broadcast.

Billy publicly spoke out about religious freedom as well, addressing the Moscow Peace Conference in 1982. He met with members of the Politburo and the Communist Party's Central Committee—bringing the authorities the names of 150 believers who had been imprisoned for practicing their Christian faith.

"The deepest problems of the human race are spiritual in nature. They are rooted in man's refusal to seek God's way for his life. The problem is the human heart, which God alone can change." ~ *Billy Graham*

CIVIL RIGHTS IN THE UNITED STATES

Although he grew up in the South in its heyday of racial segregation, Billy found nothing to support it in the Scriptures. "The ground is level at the foot of the cross," he said.

Billy desegregated all his crusades. Two years before the landmark Supreme Court decision that banned racial discrimination, he took his first steps toward integration by taking down the ropes that separated people by race. There, at the 1952 crusade in Jackson, Mississippi, 362,300 people sat side by side, regardless of skin color.

Billy's Chattanooga, Tennessee, crusade a year later was the first to be integrated from the planning stage. He instructed that participants "must be allowed to sit anywhere," overruling protests and ignoring forecasts of trouble. Though few blacks attended, those who came had their choice of seats.

Billy was so committed to racial reconciliation that he cancelled several European engagements to visit some of the South's worst trouble spots. When racial tension hit Little Rock in 1957, he offered to hold a crusade there, but the local committee thought the timing was wrong. Two years later, the crusade finally took place. Afterward, the editor of a local paper wrote Billy: "That meeting has done more [to promote racial harmony] than any single thing that has happened in Little Rock."

"Had it not been for the ministry of my good friend Dr. Billy Graham, my work in the civil rights movement would not have been as successful as it has been." ∾ *Martin Luther King Jr.*

"The most segregated hour of the week in America is the eleven o'clock Sunday morning Christian church service. It is natural for churches to organize and function along ethnic and nationalistic lines. . . . The sin comes when a church becomes exclusive and certain groups are refused admission or fellowship in worship because of race or color." ∾ *Billy Graham*, Reader's Digest, *August 1960*

ABOVE: *Martin Luther King Jr. credited Billy with having a major role in lessening tensions between the races.*

OPPOSITE: *Billy's tour of the deep South ended in June 1965 with an eight-day meeting at the Cramton Bowl in Montgomery, Alabama.*

ABOVE: *Billy and Howard Jones faced tremendous criticism when Jones became the first black associate evangelist to serve on a crusade team.*

LEFT: *Total attendance at the March 1953 Chattanooga, Tennessee, crusade reached 283,300.*

BELOW: *Blacks, whites, men, women, and children all came forward at the Cramton Bowl in Montgomery, Alabama.*

"The race question will not be solved by demonstrations in the streets, but in the hearts of both Negro and white. There must be genuine love to replace prejudice and hate. This love can be supplied by Christ and only by Christ!" ~ *Billy Graham*

ABOVE: *Billy (right of fireplace) attended a meeting with President Nixon (left of fireplace) and black ministers in 1969.*

LEFT: *In September 1963 four black children were killed in the bombing of the 16th Street Baptist Church in Birmingham, Alabama. The incident made Birmingham the focal point of America's racial upheaval. Billy offered to bring his team to the city on the condition that the meeting was integrated. On Easter Sunday, 1964, thirty-five thousand people—half black, half white—attended the rally at Birmingham's Legion Field, making it the largest integrated gathering in the state's history at that time.*

"I wept more in Korea than in all the past several years put together. These experiences changed my life. I could never be quite the same again. . . . I felt sadder, older. I felt as though I had gone in a boy and come out a man. . . ." ∽ *Billy Graham*

LEFT: *In 1952 the Korean War was in its third, bloody winter and more than twenty-one thousand young Americans were dead. Billy wanted to spend Christmas with the troops, so he petitioned Washington and finally received permission. With full military cooperation, Billy visited and preached at the battlefront, where men stood throughout the final service on Christmas Day.*

BELOW LEFT: *In Vietnam Billy visited aircraft carriers, air bases, hospitals, and jungle outposts where soldiers, sailors, marines, and airmen stood in the hot sun, pouring rain, and ankle-deep mud to hear about God's love for them.*

BELOW: *In Poland, 1978, Billy spoke at Auschwitz's Wall of Death, where twenty thousand people were shot between 1940 and 1945.*

RIGHT AND BELOW:
In 1982 six hundred Buddhist, Shinto, Muslim, and Christian delegates from various parts of the world listened to Billy's message at the peace conference in Moscow.

"I call upon the leaders of all nations to work for peace, even when the risks seem high. I call upon Christians to pray and work for peace in whatever constructive ways are open to them. I do not believe this is only a political issue; it is a moral one as well." ~ *Billy Graham, speaking at a USSR peace conference, May 11, 1982*

RIGHT: *In 1973 the Fund provided famine relief to drought-stricken West Africa.*

BELOW: *In 1976, the Grahams toured a village in Guatemala, where an earthquake had left twelve thousand dead and one million homeless. The BGEA chartered ten jets to deliver food and medical supplies.*

BELOW RIGHT: *Samaritan's Purse and BGEA donated trailers to families left homeless by Hurricane Hugo.*

"If we are going to touch the people of our communities, we too must know their sorrows, feel for them in their temptations, stand with them in their heartbreaks." ∾ *Billy Graham*

TOP: *Funds were provided to rebuild 285 homes in Andhra Pradesh. The town was named by its residents as "Billy Graham Nagar."*

ABOVE: *Shelly Cruz lost her home in the 1989 San Francisco earthquake. As Billy toured the area, he walked over and prayed with her. Later she said, "I can never tell you how much Billy Graham's visit meant to me."*

"This cyclone which struck the coast of Andhra Pradesh in 1977 remains a nightmare experience. It caused immense damage. With the help of the Billy Graham World Relief Committee, 285 houses have been rebuilt, which are being dedicated on 29th June. My good wishes for this function being held in the village named after the well-known preacher." ∾ *Indira Gandhi, prime minister of India*

GLOBAL RELIEF EFFORTS

In 1973 Billy designated the final offering at his Minnesota crusade to be for famine relief in drought-stricken central West Africa. That seventy-seven thousand dollars was the beginning of the BGEA World Emergency Relief Fund. More than ten million dollars has been donated since the Fund's inception, with 100 percent of every dollar earmarked for assistance. The Fund has provided medical supplies and equipment, small planes, food, shelter, hospitals, and churches, which also serve as community centers for refugees. In doing so, it has brought God's love to the world in a tangible way.

One of the greatest natural disasters in the twentieth century occurred in December 1977, when a cyclone-whipped tidal wave hit India's southeast coast, destroying two hundred thousand homes and killing one hundred thousand people. Billy was preaching in India when he heard the news. Immediately, he flew into the ravaged region and watched as crews of prisoners searched for victims in the sawgrass and low thorn woods. When corpses were found, Billy prayed as the bodies were covered and burned to prevent the spread of disease.

Following Hurricane Katrina in 2005, the Billy Graham Evangelistic Association rapid response teams and Samaritan's Purse disaster relief convoys, home repair crews, and medical personnel were dispatched immediately to the Gulf states. Burdened to help in an even more personal way, Billy and Ruth—like thousands of other families across America—provided a home to a family evacuated from New Orleans until they could get back on their feet and find jobs and a new home in North Carolina.

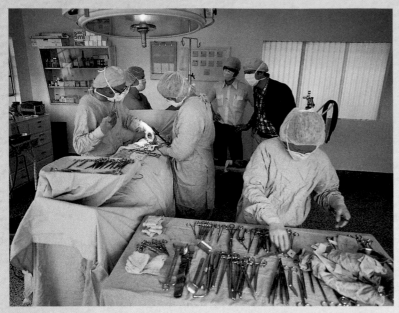

CLOCKWISE FROM TOP LEFT: *The World Emergency Relief Fund helped equip this surgical theater in Tenwek, Africa; Franklin and Billy provided Thanksgiving dinner through Franklin's organization Samaritan's Purse in Homestead, Florida, in 1992; Billy gave a food donation to the Washington, D.C., Love-in-Action committee; Associate Evangelist Howard Jones (third from right) talked with a local missionary and pastor about the food needed to stave off hunger in tiny Loul Sessene, Senegal.*

"I came here to see people. The damaged buildings you can see on television, but television can't show the damaged hearts and lives. Hopefully I can encourage them to trust in God." ∼ *Billy Graham, speaking in San Francisco*

CLOCKWISE FROM ABOVE: *Franklin Graham and Walter Smyth inspected a church in Thailand that the BGEA built to preach the love of God and to serve as a community center for Cambodian refugees; after the 1989 San Francisco earthquake, Billy walked through pouring rain to visit families in Watsonville whose homes had been destroyed and who were sheltered in tents provided by the Salvation Army; the BGEA provided funds to transport food and medical supplies to remote jungle areas in Kenya, Africa.*

Times of Tragedy

From the devastating aftermath of Hurricane Hugo in 1989 to the Oklahoma City bombing in 1995, Billy reached out to millions of people during some of America's most traumatic events. Then on September 11, 2001, the worst terrorist attack on American soil occurred when terrorists hijacked four planes and crashed them into the World Trade Center in New York City, the Pentagon in Langley, Virginia, and a field in southern Pennsylvania, killing 2,749 people. The same day, Billy prayed for the nation, saying, "Our heartfelt prayers and sympathy go out to all who have been directly touched by this tragedy, and their families. . . . If there ever was a time for us to turn to God and to pray as a nation, it is now, that this evil will spread no further."

Despite a temporary ban on flights, on September 14, 2001, the U.S. government made arrangements for Billy to fly to Washington, D.C. Billy spoke at the National Day of Prayer and Remembrance at the National Cathedral. Speaking to a stunned nation, he urged his listeners to turn to God in times of doubt and struggle: "This event reminds us of the brevity and uncertainty of life. We never know when we too will be called into eternity. . . . And that's why each of us needs to face our own spiritual need and commit ourselves to God and His will now."

Several weeks later, Franklin and the BGEA staff flew to New York City. There, they opened the Billy Graham New York Prayer Center, where pastors and other Christian workers answered thousands of phone calls, providing counsel and prayer. Teams of workers also went on the streets of Manhattan to pray and read Scripture with New Yorkers.

TOP: *In 1995 a terrorist attack demolished the Alfred P. Murrah Federal Building in Oklahoma City, Oklahoma.*

ABOVE: *Franklin met with one of the workers at Ground Zero in New York City.*

OPPOSITE: *Billy shared words of hope and faith at the National Day of Prayer and Remembrance on September 14, 2001.*

"But today, we especially come together in this service to confess our need of God. We've always needed God from the very beginning of this nation, but today we need Him especially. We're facing a new kind of enemy. We're involved in a new kind of warfare and we need the help of the Spirit of God. The Bible's words are our hope: 'God is our refuge and strength, an ever-present help in trouble. Therefore we will not fear, though the earth give way and the mountains fall into the heart of the sea'" (Psalm 46: 1–2). ∽ *Billy Graham*

"As Christians we have a responsibility toward the poor, the oppressed, the downtrodden, and the many innocent people around the world who are caught in wars, natural disasters, and situations beyond their control." ~ *Billy Graham*

In 1977, when tidal wave survivors from various villages greeted Billy in Andhra Pradesh, India, he was moved to tears—and to take action through the BGEA World Emergency Relief Fund.

Chapter Five

Inspiring Others

Throughout more than five decades of tremendous social change and upheaval, Billy's ministry played out on a large and visible stage. He met with world leaders, journalists, and ordinary citizens, guiding and comforting them as they worked through the civil rights movement, political assassinations, and even terrorist attacks.

His ultimate desire, however, was to lead one individual at a time to a personal relationship with Jesus Christ. "Whether the story of Christ is told in a huge stadium, across the desk of a powerful leader, or shared with a golfing companion, it satisfies a common hunger," Billy said. "All over the world, whenever I meet people face-to-face, I am made aware of this personal need among the famous and successful, as well as the lonely and obscure."

Every U.S. president, from Harry Truman to George W. Bush, found occasion to call on Billy. Both Lyndon Johnson and Richard Nixon, the two with whom he was probably closest, offered him high positions in government, which he quickly and politely refused. Billy was also close with many figures in sports and entertainment.

But most of his time was spent with ordinary people. Billy found that all people, famous or not, ask the same basic questions of life: Who am I? Where did I come from? Where am I going? Is there meaning in my life? He addressed these issues both in his crusades and in one-on-one meetings with individuals, reminding them that in the end, "Only God can give us the ultimate answer to those questions."

OPPOSITE: *Billy offered a warm heart, a listening ear, and encouraging comments to President Lyndon Johnson at the 1966 National Prayer Breakfast in Washington, D.C.*

BELOW: *Billy counted many famous people as his friends, and with every meeting, he made an effort to bring the conversation around to the Gospel of Jesus Christ.*

Harry S Truman

In 1950 a congressman arranged for Billy to meet the president in Washington. Without any briefing on protocol, Billy went in with three colleagues and spoke with President Truman, who told Billy he lived by the Sermon on the Mount. Billy recalled, "[Before leaving] I put my arm around him and I said, 'Could we pray?' And of course that was taking advantage of the president's graciousness in receiving us. He replied, 'Well I don't see any harm.' And so I prayed with him."

When Billy got outside, the press surrounded him, asking for pictures and an interview. Innocently, Billy told them what he had said and then posed on the White House lawn, "kneeling in prayer, like a fool," as he later recounted. God taught Billy a great lesson. A few days later, a columnist reported that President Truman had called Billy "persona non grata at the White House" because he had shared their conversation with the press. "It was a terrible mistake on my part," Billy said, "and from then on I knew that you do not quote famous people."

Years later Truman warmly received Billy at his Independence, Missouri, home, and together they laughed over the evangelist's youthful indiscretion.

ABOVE: *It wasn't until days after his meeting with Harry Truman that Billy realized his gaffe when quoting the president without authorization. Years later, he apologized. "Don't worry about it," President Truman graciously replied. "I realized you hadn't been properly briefed."*

BELOW: *Billy met with former president Truman in 1967 at Truman's home in Independence, Missouri.*

ABOVE: *President Eisenhower encouraged Billy to call him "Ike." But Billy reflected, "I never could do that. It was 'Mr. President' when he was in office, and 'General' when he was not."*

BELOW RIGHT: *Mamie and President Eisenhower talked with Billy and Dr. Ed Elson at the National Presbyterian Church in Washington, D.C., in 1953.*

DWIGHT D. EISENHOWER

34TH PRESIDENT OF THE UNITED STATES, 1953–1961

During Eisenhower's presidential campaign, Billy recommended that he and his wife join a church. "If I join a church now," Eisenhower said, "people will think I'm doing it to get votes, but I promise I will join a church whether I win or lose." After his inauguration, Eisenhower kept his word and joined the National Presbyterian Church, attending services almost every Sunday.

"Eisenhower was the first president that really asked my counsel in depth, when he was sending troops into Little Rock," Billy said. "He called me one morning in New York, where I was preaching in Madison Square Garden and said he was thinking about sending troops down there to enforce the law [against segregation]. He said, 'What do you think?' I said, 'I don't think you have an alternative; this is a terrible thing.'"

Just before Eisenhower died, Billy saw him in the hospital. "Eisenhower had his normal, big smile," Billy recollected. "He knew he didn't have long to live. He said, 'Billy, I want you to tell me once again how I can be sure my sins are forgiven and that I'm going to heaven, because nothing else matters now.'"

Billy took out his Bible and read several verses, telling the former president that he could rest knowing that Jesus' death on the cross had paid for all his—and the world's—sins. Then Billy prayed for him and held his hand. When Billy was done, Eisenhower said with a smile, "Thank you. I'm ready."

"Billy and I were riding in a car to a private luncheon with two high-ranking U.S. government officials. As we passed security and drove toward the house, Billy said he felt it would be better if we did not take any pictures. I explained that we had obtained permission, but Billy repeated his wish. He was afraid his hosts might think he was only interested in being photographed with them and that it might also interfere if he had an opportunity to talk about spiritual issues. Naturally, I waited in the car with the driver." ∾*Russ Busby, Billy's long-time photographer*

JOHN F. KENNEDY

35TH PRESIDENT OF THE UNITED STATES, 1961–1963

Four days before his inauguration, John Kennedy invited Billy to join him in Palm Beach. When Billy arrived, he met Kennedy's father, Ambassador Joseph Kennedy. "[When] I was in Stuttgart, Germany, with the president of Notre Dame University," the ambassador said, "we saw signs all over town that you were speaking at the football stadium. We decided to go out and see what it was like. We saw sixty thousand people there. We told the pope about it a few days later. The pope said, 'Yes, I wish we had a hundred Billy Grahams!' I came back and told Jack, 'One of the first things you have got to do is get in touch with Billy Graham, because you had this religion problem during the campaign between the Catholics and Protestants and I believe he can help heal it.'"

"We drove around in JFK's white Lincoln convertible," Billy remembered. "During our conversations, I became aware that he was concerned about the moral and spiritual condition of the nation. He was especially concerned about the scars that might have been left by the intense religious issue during the presidential campaign. He asked me a number of questions about the Bible. . . . That was the beginning of a friendship."

During Kennedy's funeral service in the Capitol rotunda, Billy stood about thirty feet from the Kennedy family. Billy recalled, "I could not help but think of the brevity of life. I am convinced that we need a new awareness of the fact that death is rapidly approaching for each of us and that the Bible has many warnings for us to prepare to meet God."

"Hearing from you who [have] accomplished so much good for so many people around the world is greatly appreciated. The president greatly admired you and what you are doing." ~ *Robert Kennedy,* *in a handwritten note to Billy after President Kennedy's funeral*

ABOVE: **Billy and President Kennedy enjoyed a lighthearted moment at a National Prayer Breakfast.**

RIGHT: **President Kennedy's body lay in state in the Capitol rotunda.**

President Kennedy (far left) and Vice President Johnson (far right) listened intently as Billy addressed the 1963 National Prayer Breakfast, less than a year before the president's tragic death.

"President Johnson was an outgoing sort of person. When I went to Washington and stayed in a hotel, if he found out about it, he'd call right up and say, '[There will] be a car there in fifteen minutes. Your hotel is over here.' And I'd move over to the White House." ∾ *Billy Graham*

TOP: *Billy often visited President Johnson at the White House.*

ABOVE: *Ruth, Billy, President Johnson, Lady Bird Johnson, and Lynda Johnson entered the First Christian Church in Washington where Billy preached at Johnson's inaugural prayer service.*

LYNDON B. JOHNSON

36TH PRESIDENT OF THE UNITED STATES, 1963–1969

There was a religious side to Lyndon Johnson. He was the first sitting president to attend a Graham crusade, and his family had strong spiritual roots. Often, when Billy was visiting him at the family ranch or the White House—where Billy spent more than twenty nights during Johnson's administration—he and Billy talked in his bedroom late at night. Each time they prayed together, the president would get out of bed and kneel.

Of all the presidents, Billy was probably closest to Johnson. "I saw the workings of the presidency and the White House through him more than any other president," Billy said.

The weekend before the 1964 Democratic convention, Ruth and Billy dined alone with President and Mrs. Johnson. That night, the president asked for Billy's input on a list of fourteen vice-presidential candidates. Ruth promptly kicked Billy under the table. Comfortable among their longtime friends, Billy looked at her and said, "Ruth, why did you kick me?"

"Mr. President," Ruth said to Johnson, "I think that he ought to give you only spiritual counsel, and not political counsel."

The president agreed, but later, after Ruth and Mrs. Johnson had left the room, he said to Billy, "All right, tell me who you really think."

Billy suggested Hubert Humphrey. "I think he'd already made up his mind," Billy said, "but he did choose Hubert Humphrey."

LEFT: *Billy enjoyed many moments with President Johnson at the LBJ ranch. He described his good friend as "a very rough and very tough man with his staff and other people. On occasion he would use pretty rough language, even in front of a clergy-man, though he would always say, 'Pardon me, Reverend.'"*

BELOW LEFT: *The Johnsons and Grahams were longtime friends.*

BELOW: *On January 25, 1973, Billy spoke at the president's funeral under the old oak tree. "Lyndon Johnson was a mountain of a man with a whirlwind for a heart," he said.*

"My mind went back to those lonely occasions at the White House when your friendship helped to sustain a president in an hour of trial. . . . No one will ever know how you helped to lighten my load or how much warmth you brought into our house. But I know." ∾ *Lyndon Johnson, in a personal letter to Billy shortly after leaving office*

RICHARD M. NIXON

37TH PRESIDENT OF THE UNITED STATES, 1969–1974

President Nixon and Billy had been personal friends since 1950. From the very beginning of their friendship Billy said, "I realized he had one of the most brilliant minds I was ever to know."

Though Nixon was a private and complex person, beneath the surface Billy found him to be warm and compassionate, quite different from the popular caricatures of him. He often answered letters from friends with a handwritten reply. "He was a strong family man," Billy remembered, "and I have never known anyone who was more devoted to his wife or to his children and their families."

Nixon was also a man of genuine faith, rooted in the prayers and teachings of his devout Quaker mother. Often he had Billy pray with him and read the Bible to him when they would visit. Nixon usually listened in silence—as a Quaker, he kept his piety private. Except for saying grace at mealtimes, he did not pray out loud.

Right before the Watergate scandal broke, Billy noticed that Nixon was not himself. "He did not look well at all," said Billy. "His eyes betrayed that something was wrong." Billy had no idea, however, of the scandal that was about to unfold; Nixon never confided in him about it. In fact, after the story broke, Billy could not get near the president or even talk with his secretary or his children. Later he learned that Nixon had ordered his staff to keep Billy away. "I am convinced that he was trying to spare me from being tarred with Watergate," Billy reflected.

When Nixon died in 1994, Billy greeted the family members, American presidents, and other distinguished guests at the funeral. During the service, he preached, "For the person who has turned from sin and has received Christ as Lord and Savior, death is not the end. . . . Richard Nixon had that hope, and today that can be our hope as well."

TOP: *Ruth, Pat Nixon, Billy, and President Nixon joined the singing at the 1970 Knoxville crusade.*

ABOVE: *Richard Nixon visited Billy and Ruth at their home in the 1960s.*

"There comes a moment when we all must realize that life is short, and in the end the only thing that really counts is not how others see us, but how God sees us. For the believer there is hope beyond the grave, because Jesus Christ has opened the door to heaven for us by His death and resurrection." ∼ *Billy Graham, speaking at Richard Nixon's funeral*

ABOVE: *Billy spoke at Nixon's funeral in 1994.*

LEFT: *Presidents Clinton, Bush, Reagan, Carter, and Ford (with their wives) attended the memorial service for Richard Nixon.*

GERALD R. FORD

38TH PRESIDENT OF THE UNITED STATES, 1974–1977

Gerald Ford had served in the House of Representatives since the Truman days. When he took the oath of office as President of the United States, he said to the American people in his inaugural address, "I am acutely aware that you have not elected me as your president by your ballots, so I ask you to confirm me as your president with your prayers. . . . Let us restore the Golden Rule to our political process. And let brotherly love purge our hearts of suspicion and of hate. . . ."

Like those before him, Ford enjoyed a long friendship with Billy. Some criticized his relationship with the evangelist, but Ford simply said, "I've heard the comments from some sources that Billy mixes politics with religion. I never felt that and I don't think that the thousands and thousands of people who listen to him felt that.

"Billy dropped by the Oval Office on several occasions while I was president," Ford continued. "They were get-togethers of old friends. They had no political or other significance. It was simply an expression, or an extension, of our long-standing friendship."

"I agreed with [Ford's] presidential pardon [of Nixon] because I believe that the trial of a former president would be destructive and not in the best interests of the nation. A one- or two-year trial would tear America apart." ∽ *Billy Graham*

TOP: *Billy visited President Ford at the White House in the mid-1970s.*

ABOVE: *Billy joined President Ford at a pro-am tournament in Charlotte, North Carolina, in 1974.*

JIMMY CARTER

39TH PRESIDENT OF THE UNITED STATES,
1977–1981

In 1966 staff members from the Billy Graham Evangelistic Association went to Americus, Georgia, to hold a film crusade. Billy needed a chairman who would hold integrated meetings, which he demanded for all of his work. "Jimmy Carter was the only man who had the courage to be the chairman," Billy said. "That was before Carter ever ran for any political office. Then when Jimmy was governor of Georgia he was the honorary chairman of our Atlanta crusade."

Carter remembered, "When I was asked to head up a Billy Graham evangelical program in Sumter County, in strict segregation days . . . I told the planning groups they would have to be integrated. . . . And when I went to the major churches, none of them would let us come in. So we went to the basement of an abandoned school building and that's where we had our integrated planning meetings. And then the Billy Graham films were shown in our local theater."

"Billy and Ruth Graham have been to visit us both in the governor's mansion in Georgia and in the White House. His reputation is above reproach or suspicion. He's been a Christlike figure with a globally beneficial impact in evangelism."

~ *Jimmy Carter*

ABOVE: *Governor and Rosalynn Carter attended the 1973 crusade in Atlanta Stadium.*

RIGHT: *Following a White House visit, Billy and Ruth received this memento.*

To our good friends Ruth & Billy Graham
Jimmy Carter   Rosalynn Carter

"I appreciated Billy Graham being on hand at a time that was rather difficult. I remember that I wanted him to know that I had called on the Almighty for help and [asked that] if He did not have some other plan, then I would recover and regain my health. But I didn't think I could call on God for help without saying that whatever life was left for me belonged to Him." ∾ *Ronald Reagan, on the 1981 assassination attempt*

ABOVE: *Nancy and Governor Reagan joined Billy at the 1969 Anaheim crusade.*

RONALD W. REAGAN

40TH PRESIDENT OF THE UNITED STATES, 1981–1989

Billy met Ronald Reagan a year after Reagan married Nancy. Nancy's mother introduced the two men, saying to Billy, "I want you to get to know my new son-in-law, Ronald Reagan." Billy said, "You mean the film star?" She said, "Yes."

The two men connected and remained close friends over the years. "I remember," Billy often reminisced, "when Reagan was president of the Screen Actors Guild, a union leader—and a very strong Democrat!"

On March 30, 1981, after the attempt on President Reagan's life, Billy flew immediately to Washington, D.C., to comfort and pray with Mrs. Reagan and do anything he could for the president. Billy later contacted the father of John Hinckley Jr., the president's assailant, and prayed with him over the telephone.

Four years later, at the beginning of Reagan's second term, Billy spoke at the National Prayer Service. "During the next four years," he said, "many of you here today will have to make decisions of state perhaps greater than any of those made by your predecessors. Because of modern technology, you will hold in your hands the destiny not only of America but of the entire world. Christ, whom the Bible speaks of as the source of all wisdom, said, 'What shall it profit a man if he shall gain the whole world, and lose his own soul?' (Mark 8:36). I believe that applies to nations as well as individuals, for a nation that loses its spiritual courage will grow old before its time."

"It was through Billy Graham that I found myself praying even more than on a daily basis . . . and that in the position I held [of president], that my prayers more and more were to give me the wisdom to make decisions that would serve God and be pleasing to Him." ~ *Ronald Reagan*

ABOVE: *Billy and Ruth enjoyed a visit at the White House with Nancy and President Reagan.*

LEFT: *Billy and the Reagans went back a long way. This photo was taken shortly after they met.*

Billy Graham greeted President and Nancy Reagan in Washington, D.C., during the National Prayer Breakfast in February 1981.

"Billy Graham has been an inspiration in my life. It is my firm belief that no one can be president without a belief in God, without understanding the power of prayer, without faith. And Billy Graham helped me understand that. . . . I thank God for bringing Billy Graham into the lives of my family. He gave us great strength, and through him we better know God's Son, Jesus Christ." ～ *George H. W. Bush*

GEORGE H. W. BUSH

41ST PRESIDENT OF THE UNITED STATES, 1989–1993

ABOVE: **Billy and President Bush enjoyed fishing together off the coast of Maine.**

Billy and Ruth were longtime friends of the Bushes. Billy knew President Bush's mother and father, and Billy and Ruth sometimes joined the president and his family at Kennebunkport. "They are an incredible family," Billy said. "Ruth often said that it's worth having George Bush as president to get Barbara as first lady."

Although close friends, they never spoke about public affairs, instead focusing on spiritual issues. Billy found the elder Bush easy to talk to about God, "easier than other presidents I have met," he said. "He says straight out that he has received Christ as his Savior, that he is a born-again believer, and that he reads the Bible daily. He has the highest moral standards of almost anybody whom I have known. He and his wife have such a relationship—it is just unbelievable. If you are with them in private, you know, they are just like lovers."

On January 16, 1991, Billy was called to the White House. When he arrived, Mrs. Bush invited him to the Blue Room to watch the news. Without her saying a word, the look on her face told him that it was the beginning of Operation Desert Storm. About thirty minutes later the president came in. Billy knew President Bush had spent a great deal of time in prayer and meditation over this decision. "We had prayer and talked a long time," Billy said. "During our conversation he said, 'Would you do something for me?' I said, 'Yes.' He said, 'I would like to call Mr. Cheney, General Powell, and the leadership of our top military together tomorrow morning and have you speak to them.'" Billy readily agreed, praying for all sides in the conflict.

ABOVE: *Billy delivered the prayer at President Bush's inauguration on January 20, 1989, in Washington, D.C.*

RIGHT: *Billy visited President and Barbara Bush at the White House in January 1991, when the Gulf War began.*

FAR RIGHT: *Billy and Ruth visited President and Barbara Bush and President Bush's mother, Dorothy, at Kennebunkport, Maine, in the early 1990s.*

To the Grahams from the Kennebunkport Bushes with love— Geo. Bush & Barbara

WILLIAM J. CLINTON

42ND PRESIDENT OF THE UNITED STATES,
1993–2001

President Clinton once recalled, "When I was a small boy, about twelve years old, Billy Graham came to Little Rock, Arkansas, to preach a crusade. Our town was torn apart by racial conflict. Our high schools were closed, and there were those who asked Billy Graham to segregate his audience in War Memorial Stadium, so as not to roil the waters.

"I'll never forget what he said—that if he had to speak the Word of God to a segregated audience he would violate his ministry, and he would not do it. And at the most intense time in the modern history of my state, everybody caved, and blacks and whites together poured into the football stadium. And when the invitation was given, they poured down the aisles together, and they forgot they were supposed to be mad at each other, and angry at each other, that one was supposed to consider the other somehow less than equal.

"He never preached a word about integrating the schools. He preached the Word of God, and he lived it by the power of his example. And one young boy from a modest family for a long time thereafter took just a little money out of his allowance every month and sent it to the Billy Graham crusade."

ABOVE: *Governor Bill Clinton joined Billy at the Little Rock crusade, September 1989.*

OPPOSITE: *Billy and President Clinton shared a private moment in the Oval Office.*

"Billy and Ruth Graham have practiced the ministry of . . . being friends with presidents of both parties, counseling them in countless ways, always completely private, always completely genuine. . . . We sat in the Oval Office reminiscing and talking about current circumstances, and I asked for Billy Graham's prayers for the wisdom and guidance of God." ∼*Bill Clinton*

GEORGE W. BUSH

43RD PRESIDENT OF THE UNITED STATES,
2001–2009

Unlike his relationships with other presidents, Billy's friendship with George W. Bush began when the president was just a child. In fact, the Grahams' ties with the Bush family spanned four generations—from Senator Prescott Bush to George W. Bush's daughters, Barbara and Jenna.

Billy's example of faith dramatically changed the course of George W. Bush's life. In his autobiography, Bush recalled: "[The Reverend Billy Graham] visited my family for a summer weekend in Maine. . . . One evening my dad asked Billy to answer questions from a big group of family gathered for the weekend. He sat by the fire and talked. And what he said sparked a change in my heart. . . . It was the beginning of a new walk where I would commit my heart to Jesus Christ."

Billy's relationship with Bush continued throughout his political career. As governor of Texas, the younger Bush served as honorary chair of Billy's 1997 San Antonio Crusade. There, he addressed the crowd, saying fondly, "Dr. Graham is a rare human being whose insights in the faith have had an enormous influence over all our lives. More than a decade ago he helped change my own life in a personal and profound way. Knowing him as a friend has been one of the greatest honors of my life."

TOP: *Billy and Franklin Graham met with George and Laura Bush at the Jacksonville crusade in Florida during the fall of 2000 prior to President Bush's election.*

ABOVE: *Franklin led the country in prayer at President Bush's inauguration in 2001.*

ABOVE: *Billy with President George W. Bush at a White House dinner in 2001 celebrating Billy's eighty-third birthday.*

"I knew I was in the presence of a great man. He was like a magnet—I felt drawn to make changes in my life. He didn't lecture or admonish; he shared warmth and concern. Billy Graham didn't make you feel guilty; he made you feel loved."

∼ *George W. Bush*

MEETINGS WITH WORLD LEADERS

Throughout his ministry, Billy had the opportunity to meet with many of the world's leaders and visionaries. From heads of state to religious leaders, many testify to his wise counsel, noting that he added a moral perspective to their thinking. Leaders also appreciated Billy's respect for their privacy and the fact that he did not approach them with a personal agenda. President Ford attested to this, saying, "Billy made many, many contributions to our society across the board and because of his inspirational abilities, he was able to influence millions and millions of people. . . . His interest was in social justice—Billy Graham spoke from the heart, from the Bible, and from his own conviction on social issues that were on the agenda at the time."

ABOVE LEFT: *Billy and Ruth socialized with Secretary of State Henry Kissinger in 1973.*

ABOVE: *In 1984 Queen Elizabeth II, Prince Philip, and the Queen Mother welcomed Billy and Ruth to Sandringham, where he preached in the chapel.*

LEFT: *In 1951 Billy met with President Syngman Rhee of South Korea.*

"Billy Graham doesn't give you tactical advice on what to do politically. He talks about the moral dimension of the issues. And the reason world leaders have sought his advice is precisely because he doesn't try to tell them what they should do tomorrow. But he does try to show them a way of thinking about the problem that adds a new dimension to their thinking."

~ *Henry Kissinger,* Secretary of State

"Billy Graham is a great teacher in all the important matters to humanity, and a dear friend of Israel."
~ *Golda Meir*

"I had a long talk with the chief rabbi in Israel. I asked him if he believed in the coming of the Messiah, and he assured me that he did. I told him that I, too, believe in the coming of the Messiah, but that when the Messiah comes we will all recognize that He is Jesus who was on earth once before. The chief rabbi smiled over his cup of coffee and said, 'Of course, that's our difference.'" ~ *Billy Graham*

TOP: *With Prime Minister Golda Meir, Israel, 1969*

ABOVE LEFT TO RIGHT: *Meeting King Hussein Jordan, 1960; with comedian and golfer Bob Hope; and with President Kim Il Sung, North Korea, 1992*

"I've played many rounds of golf with Billy. We're a lot alike. He prays and I cheat. He cheats in his own pious way. I mean, how would you like to play eighteen holes and have it raining just on you? He always wins." ~ *Bob Hope*

"When I arrived at the airport, Mr. Graham himself was waiting for me. I expected to be chauffeured in a Rolls Royce or at least a Mercedes, but we got in his Oldsmobile and he drove it himself. I couldn't believe he came to the airport driving his own car. When we approached his home I thought he would live on a thousand-acre farm, and we drove up to this house made of logs. No mansion with crystal chandeliers and gold carpets. It was the kind of house a man of God would live in. I look up to him."

~ *Muhammad Ali*

CLOCKWISE FROM TOP LEFT: *With Pope John Paul II, 1993; meeting with Prime Minister Indira Gandhi in India, 1973; with General Secretary Mikhail* *Gorbachev at the Kremlin, 1991; with Premier Li Peng in China, 1988; and with Muhammad Ali at the Grahams' mountain-top home in 1979*

"During all my years as an evangelist, my message has always been the Gospel of Christ. It is not a Western religion, nor is it a message of one culture or political system. . . . It is a message of life and hope for all the world." ∼ *Billy Graham*

CLOCKWISE FROM TOP LEFT: *With President Jose Lopez Portillo, Mexico, 1981; British Prime Minister Margaret Thatcher,* *1989; Coretta Scott King, 1987; and President François Mitterand, France, 1986*

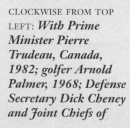

CLOCKWISE FROM TOP LEFT: *With Prime Minister Pierre Trudeau, Canada, 1982; golfer Arnold Palmer, 1968; Defense Secretary Dick Cheney and Joint Chiefs of* *Staff Chairman General Colin Powell, 1991; filmmaker and theme park designer Walt Disney, 1966; and Vice President Daniel Arap-Moi, Kenya, 1976*

"Billy Graham, a prophet in our time, reaches an amazing range of people. His message crosses all barriers which traditionally separate our societies and nations into the have-nots, the powerful and the weak, the affluent and the poor, the liberal and the conservative, and the religious divisions of denominations and faiths." ~ *Reverend Ernest Gibson, Washington, D.C.*

FROM TOP: *Billy appeared with Jane Pauley, Tom Brokaw, and Willard Scott on the* Today *show in 1981; Billy was interviewed in 1968 by Barbara Walters and Hugh Downs; Billy enjoyed a light moment with Peter Jennings in 1996.*

OPPOSITE: *Billy spoke at a New York City press conference in 1969.*

"No man could be so continually surrounded for so many years with so much adulation and criticism, and still remain the plainly decent, good-humored, thoughtfully kind man he is, without being of quality timber." ∽ *George Cornell, Associated Press*

THE POWER OF THE MEDIA

Billy always utilized the media to extend the reach of his message, sharing the Gospel in newspaper, radio, television, and the Internet. When Billy first attracted media attention in the late 1940s, the secular journalists sent to cover his crusades were in unfamiliar territory. They were not used to covering evangelism, and some didn't understand the evangelical language. Reporters needed some clear definitions, so the Graham team provided a glossary of religious terms. The team also arranged for press conferences, allowing Billy to give reporters a better understanding of his ministry. Billy always made sure his presentations were simple and, thus, effective.

Their efforts went a long way. When the Associated Press assigned George Cornell to cover Billy's 1957 New York crusade, Cornell broke new ground as a regular religion reporter. Soon there were many full-time religion writers for American newspapers.

"So many people think that somehow I carry a revival around in a suitcase, and they just announce me and something happens— but that's not true. This is the work of God, and the Bible warns that God will not share His glory with another. All the publicity that we receive sometimes frightens me because I feel that therein lies a great danger. If God should take His hand off me, I would have no more spiritual power. The whole secret of the success of our meetings is spiritual—it's God answering prayer. I cannot take credit for any of it." ∽ *Billy Graham*

"He has walked with royalty and received unprecedented media attention for over four decades but is still something of a small-town boy, astonished that anyone would think him special. In a profession stained by scandal, he stands out as the clearly identified exemplar of clean-living integrity. In a society divided by divorce, he and the wife of his youth have reared five attractive and capable children, all of whom are faithful Christians. He is, in short, an authentic American hero."

~ *Bill Martin,* author of A Prophet with Honor: The Billy Graham Story

"I am just a spectator watching what God is doing." ~ *Billy Graham*

"Billy hasn't changed a bit; he's like he always was. Billy's way of speaking and his personality are an advantage, but the real drawing power is the power of God."

~ *Melvin Graham, Billy's brother*

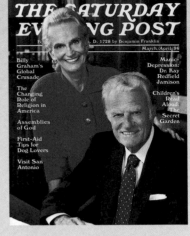

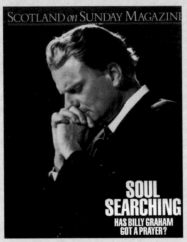

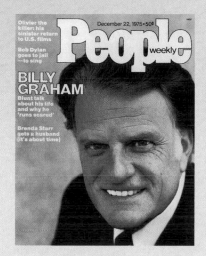

"Everywhere I go I find that people . . . both leaders and individuals . . . are asking one basic question: 'Is there any hope for the future? Is there any hope for peace, justice, and prosperity in our generation?'" ∾ *Billy Graham, on the existence of God*, U.S. News & World Report, *April 25, 1966*

"There is a God. God is not 'dead.' There are many evidences pointing to the fact that there is a God, but I don't think that we can draw a scientific conclusion. We can't go to a laboratory and demonstrate Him. . . . Of course, the ultimate step, it seems to me, has to be by faith that there is a God."

∾ *Billy Graham, in response to a journalist's question about the existence of God*, U.S. News & World Report, *April 25, 1966*

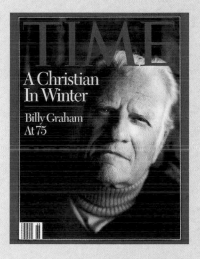

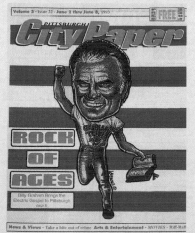

"I believe that in each generation God raises up certain people He can trust with success. I would put Billy in line with the Wesleys and Saint Augustine and Francis of Assisi. He's in that league. And what's extraordinary is that he doesn't seem to know it."

∾ *Reverend Maurice Wood, bishop of Norwich and member of Britain's House of Lords*

Billy looked at every chance to be in magazines or in newspapers as an opportunity to share the Good News. His humble attitude brought him more print space and more favorable editorials as time went on.

ABOVE: *Following his return from the Soviet Union, Billy faced reporters at a 1984 press conference in New York City.*

FAR LEFT: *Russian media interviewed Billy aboard an Aeroflot flight in 1984.*

LEFT: *With Dan Rather, 1979*

"It is strange how one has become used to publicity. I used to strongly resent the invasion of our privacy; now I have learned to live with it and have dedicated it to the Lord." ～ *Billy Graham*

"It is good to have Billy Graham around, for things start happening much for the better in ordinary people's lives." ～ *John Knight*, Sunday Mirror, *London*

"He has accomplished so many things, inspired so many people, changed so many lives. His message of hope is still ringing, his legacy is everlasting." ~ *Jim Hunt, governor of North Carolina*

TOP: *Being interviewed by Larry King on* **Larry King Live,** *1994*

ABOVE LEFT: *Billy has answered questions at press conferences all over the world, including this one in* *a smoke-filled room at the Birmingham, Alabama, crusade in 1972.*

ABOVE: *Billy prayed before his CNN interview in 1993.*

Honors and Awards

During his more than sixty years of preaching to the world, Billy Graham was named Most Admired, Most Photographed, and Man of the Year. He was inducted into Halls of Fame and given Medals of Honor; he was named Honorary Sheriff, Honorary Citizen, Grand Marshal, and Salesman of the Year; and he was awarded doctoral degrees by institutions of higher learning in the United States and several foreign countries.

Cities across the United States proclaimed Billy Graham Days to honor him for coming to their areas to preach. Nigerians named a mountain for Billy that he climbed when he preached in their area. Citizens of South India named a town for him after he came to the aid of thousands who had been devastated by a tidal wave. And his birthplace of Charlotte, North Carolina, named a freeway in his honor.

Religious groups of all types—from Roman Catholics to Jews to the members of the B'nai B'rith—also bestowed awards upon Billy for his contribution to religious tolerance. And the U.S. government recognized him for his contributions to race relations. In 1963 New York senator Jacob Javits presented him with a Gold Award of the George Washington Carver Memorial Institute. More than three decades later, in May 1996, he and Ruth were awarded the Congressional Gold Medal, the highest honor the U.S. Congress can bestow upon a citizen.

But Billy remained humble. "I cannot take credit," he would say, "for what God has chosen to accomplish through us and our ministry. Only God deserves the glory."

"Billy Graham's contribution to the well-being of mankind is literally immeasurable. Millions of lives across the globe have been enriched because of his good work. The world is a better place because of Billy Graham." ∽ *Ronald Reagan, presenting the Presidential Medal of Freedom to Billy Graham, February 23, 1983*

"All that I have been able to do I owe to Jesus Christ. When you honor me you are really honoring Him. Any honors I have received I accept with a sense of inadequacy and humility and I will reserve the right to hand all of these someday to Christ, when I see Him face-to-face."

∽ *Billy Graham*

OPPOSITE: **President Reagan awarded the Presidential Medal of Freedom to Billy for his "exceptional contributions to the United States on behalf of world peace."**

ABOVE LEFT: **On May 2, 1996, Billy and Ruth were honored with the Congressional Gold Medal, the highest honor that Congress can bestow.**

ABOVE: **British Ambassador Sir Christopher Meyer presented Billy with an honorary knighthood in 2001 in recognition of his services to civic and religious life.**

Tournament of Roses

ABOVE: *Billy was grand marshal of parades in several cities but one of his biggest thrills came on January 1, 1971, when he fulfilled the role in the Pasadena, California, Rose Parade.*

LEFT: *To commemorate Billy Graham Day in the evangelist's hometown, President Nixon and his wife, Pat (left of Ruth), presented a plaque to the city of Charlotte, North Carolina. When the day was over, Billy confessed to a friend, "It's too much for a country boy. I'm turning it all over to the One to whom it belongs—to the Lord. He's the One who made it possible."*

"My primary desire today in having my name inscribed upon this Walk of Fame is that God would receive the glory. I hope someday somebody will come and say, 'Who is Billy Graham? What did he stand for?' Perhaps a child will ask his parents or grandparents, and they will tell him that he was not a celebrity, not a star, but a simple preacher of the Gospel. And they might explain the Gospel to him, and that many might find Christ in that." ∾ *Billy Graham*

CLOCKWISE FROM TOP LEFT: *Father Cuthbert Allen, a Catholic, presented the 1969 Torch of Liberty Award, a Jewish award given by the Anti-Defamation League of B'nai B'rith, to Billy Graham; in 1989 Billy received the 1,900th star on Hollywood's Walk of Fame—the first clergyman to be honored for a radio, television, and film ministry; Ruth and Billy were welcomed by Governor Jim Hunt, Wayne McDevitt, and Gordon Myers in 1996 when the city of Asheville, North Carolina, named Interstate 240 after Billy.*

"People from all walks of life are searching for answers to life's problems. I believe the Bible has the answer to man's deepest needs." ∾ *Billy Graham*

Whether Billy was speaking to a crowd of thousands or with one person across a table, his mission was always the same: to help people find a personal relationship with God. And Billy's message itself never changed. "God's forgiveness is available to all of us," he said, "no matter who we are or what we've done."

~ Chapter Six ~

Reflections from Home

When Ruth met Billy at Wheaton College, she was planning to go to Tibet as a missionary. "We nearly broke up because he said God was not calling him to Tibet," she once recounted. "Finally, he asked me, 'Do you believe that God brought us together?' And I did without question."

Ruth told Billy, "God has given you the gift of evangelism, and I'll back you. I'll rear the children and you travel and preach." So instead of working the mission field of Asia, Ruth worked the mission field of her home—what she would call "one of the most challenging, difficult, and rewarding jobs in the world."

"Ruth took the major responsibility," Billy said. "I have to give her 99 percent of the credit for those children because she's the one who listened to them, wiped their tears when they cried, and helped them through the rough places. I'd come home and she had everything so organized and so calmed down. I tried to let all five children know that I loved them and that I missed them when I was away, that I supported their mother's discipline of them, and that I wanted them to discover God's perfect plan for each of them. We did all we could to encourage the children and give them memories of life together as a family that would be warm and happy.

"Without Ruth's partnership and encouragement over the years," he continued, "my own work would have been impossible. We were called by God as a team."

OPPOSITE: *Ruth and Billy, at home on their front porch, celebrated their fiftieth wedding anniversary in 1993.*

BELOW: *When the Grahams met in the early 1940s, Billy was so smitten that it took him a month to muster the courage to ask Ruth out on a date.*

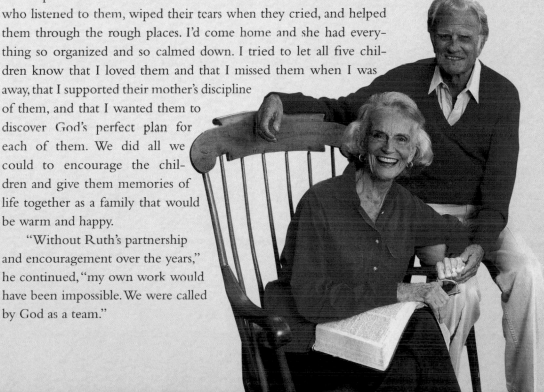

"As busy as Daddy was, he spent time with me, he loved me, he prayed with me, he cried with me, and that will always be a special memory. And I don't believe Mother has ever been recognized and honored for what she has done; because without her, Daddy's ministry would not have been possible." ∼ *Ruth "Bunny" Graham*

A SPIRITUAL LEGACY

Billy was once asked where he turned for spiritual guidance. He replied, "My wife, Ruth. Her life is ruled by the Bible more than any person I've ever known. That's her rule book, her compass. When it comes to spiritual things, she has had the greatest influence on my ministry." Indeed, she and Billy were first and foremost partners—both in ministry and in family life. Throughout her life, Ruth remained an active voice for the BGEA, writing columns for *Decision* magazine as well as penning her own books and poetry.

The Graham children, too, have carried on this legacy of evangelism. All are admired speakers, authors of multiple books, and leaders in their communities. Gigi, the eldest, speaks on issues facing today's society. Anne founded AnGeL Ministries, a Bible teaching program, and writes Bible studies for *Decision*. Ruth founded Ruth Graham Ministries in which she teaches at conferences and other international meetings. Franklin is CEO and president of the BGEA and president of Samaritan's Purse. He has conducted numerous events for the BGEA, preaching to millions of people. And Ned, the youngest, is president of East Gates Ministries International, which publishes and distributes Bibles to Christians in the People's Republic of China.

OPPOSITE: *Billy and Ruth at home in December 2006. Billy often said of his wife, "My work through the years would not have been possible without her encouragement and support."*

TOP LEFT: *Ruth published several books in her own right, including poetry and an autobiography.*

ABOVE: *Franklin, Ruth "Bunny," Anne, Gigi, Ruth, and Ned at home in Montreat, 1958.*

*Gigi, Anne, Ruth,
Ruth, Billy, Franklin,
and Ned celebrated
Ruth and Billy's
fiftieth wedding
anniversary at their
home in Montreat.*

"Knowing how long and how hard God has worked on this particular servant of His, I had to come out here and, like Moses at the burning bush, stand aside and see this great sight. In case there's some mother out there concerned for a son who is away from the Lord—let me say nobody's helpless. I mean it—nobody."

~ *Ruth Graham, speaking at Franklin's ordination*

TAKING UP THE TORCH OF MINISTRY

As president and CEO of Samaritan's Purse for the past twenty years, and CEO of the Billy Graham Evangelistic Association since 2000, Franklin Graham has taken up the torch of ministry his father left behind. His journey was not an easy one. A self-proclaimed "wild child," Franklin initially rebelled against the Graham name and the spiritual legacy he was destined to inherit. "I just wanted to have fun," Franklin said, describing his past of "drinking beer, going out to parties, and running around with different girlfriends."

The Grahams prayed unceasingly for their prodigal, trusting that God would eventually get Franklin's attention. Finally, in 1974, Franklin surrendered his life to Christ, saying, "I was tired of being tired." In 1979 he took over Samaritan's Purse from Bob Pierce. Samaritan's Purse, an international relief and evangelism organization, provides food, shelter, and medical support to suffering people throughout the world. Since the mid-1990s, Franklin has become increasingly involved with the BGEA, as vice-chairman of the board and later as CEO and president.

Franklin remains committed to the BGEA, holding his own crusades (now called "festivals") around the world and spreading God's Gospel, which his father preached all his life. Through these events, Franklin has preached to more than three million people on five continents, bringing thousands to Christ.

As Billy and Ruth's elder son, Franklin has acknowledged the tremendous influence his parents—and particularly his mother—had on his life. "To be honest," he once said, "I never would have been standing here [preaching] if Mama hadn't prayed for me all through the years."

OPPOSITE: *Ruth and Franklin at the family home in Montreat in 1993.*

TOP LEFT: *Franklin called for decisions in the rain at a festival in Sydney, Australia, 1996.*

TOP: *Ned, Billy, and Franklin in 1965*

ABOVE: *Billy and Franklin shared the stage at the turn of the twenty-first century.*

"Because of their example, I respected them and listened to their advice. I saw Daddy live what he preached. I saw them making Christ their life—not just their religion." ≈ *Gigi Graham Foreman*

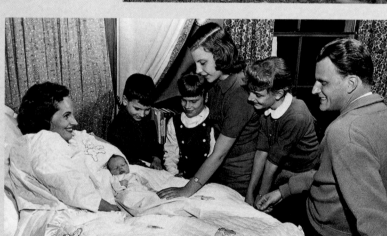

CLOCKWISE FROM TOP LEFT: *Billy and Franklin in the Grahams' front yard in 1979; Billy and Ruth "Bunny" in the 1950s; Gigi with Ruth in the kitchen; Billy and Ruth with thirteen of their grandchildren in 1982; the Graham family with four-week-old Nelson, or "Ned"*

"I know it was lonely many times for us children not having Daddy at home more, and there were times we would ask questions. But today as I travel around the world . . . I meet people who tell me they came to Christ through one of Daddy's meetings. Then I think back on those lonely times and say it was worth it all to sacrifice that time with Daddy so they could come to faith in Christ." ∾ *Franklin Graham*

CLOCKWISE FROM TOP LEFT: *Billy and Ruth on their front porch in 1972; Anne and one of the many Graham dogs, 1961; Billy and Ned in 1974; Billy and Ruth in a rare quiet moment*

"The Billy Graham the public does not know is the man confronted with thousands of invitations to preach around the world. Invitations press in on him as opportunities [and he] is forced by these and other circumstances to spend hours in prayer. There are sleepless nights and early-morning hours in Bible study."

~ **Dr. L. Nelson Bell,** *Billy's father-in-law*

CLOCKWISE FROM TOP LEFT: *Billy and Gigi, 1971; five-year-old Virginia, "Gigi," (left) and two-year-old Anne admiring baby Ruth, nicknamed "Bunny," 1950; Nelson and Virginia Bell, Ruth's parents, 1972*

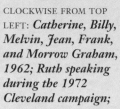

CLOCKWISE FROM TOP LEFT: *Catherine, Billy, Melvin, Jean, Frank, and Morrow Graham, 1962; Ruth speaking during the 1972 Cleveland campaign;* *the auditorium at Ruth's public funeral service in Montreat was filled to capacity with family members and friends; Morrow and Frank Graham,* *Billy's parents, in the 1960s; William Franklin Graham IV, III, and II at a 1994 crusade*

"My wife Ruth was the most incredible woman I have ever known. Whenever I was asked to name the finest Christian I ever met, I always replied, 'My wife, Ruth.' She was a spiritual giant, whose unparalleled knowledge of the Bible and commitment to prayer were a challenge and inspiration to everyone who knew her."

∼ *Billy Graham, in a tribute to Ruth at her June 2007 memorial*

"Someone asked me recently if I didn't think God was unfair, allowing me to have Parkinson's and other medical problems when I have tried to serve Him faithfully. I replied that I did not see it that way at all. Suffering is part of the human condition, and it comes to us all. The key is how we react to it, either turning away from God in anger and bitterness or growing closer to Him in trust and confidence."

~ *Billy Graham*

Billy took a much-
deserved break in
1972 before resum-
ing his traveling and
preaching. He loved
to unwind at his
family home, but his
hectic schedule seldom
allowed it.

Billy reflected that having Franklin join him in preaching the Gospel was a "fulfillment of prayer" and evidence of God's "persistent pursuit" of Franklin.

Our Continuing Ministry

When I was born, messages came to my parents from all around the world thanking God for the new evangelist He brought into the world. I was proclaimed a preacher before I could talk! No wonder I rebelled when I was younger. But gradually, my heavenly Father's calling grew too loud to ignore. After giving my life over to Jesus Christ, I began to do His work, much to the relief of my parents. My faith in God and love for my fellow man have only grown as I have worked with Samaritan's Purse and the Billy Graham Evangelistic Association. The good these ministries have accomplished by the grace of God is truly amazing.

When I was asked to be the CEO of the BGEA, I pledged to keep the focus squarely on the ministry and work of evangelism, telling people everywhere the Good News that God loves them and that Jesus Christ, His Son, died for their sins. This is the same message my father faithfully proclaimed for more than sixty years and it continues to be the central theme of our ministry.

My father was a very effective communicator who used radio, television, films, and later in his life, the Internet, to share the Lord with others. He preached tirelessly around the world, meeting with leaders of nations, hardened criminals, and those in remote places desperate to hear the love of God for them. He touched the lives of innumerable people and turned thousands to Jesus Christ.

As I have often said, the Lord called my father to the stadiums of the world and me to the ditches and gutters. (However, as time has passed, I have found myself in some of the same stadiums preaching the same Gospel message.) I have worked in those ditches through Samaritan's Purse, an international Christian relief organization that has placed hundreds of doctors in mission hospitals, brought scores of children to the U.S. for lifesaving heart surgery, and delivered tens of millions of gift-filled shoe boxes to underprivileged children around the world at Christmas. Please pray with me that God will continue to guide our every step at the BGEA and Samaritan's Purse so that the Good News of God's love can be proclaimed around the world.

The Lord Jesus Christ commanded His disciples to preach the Gospel until He comes again. My father did just that for over half a century, and I am proud to continue that work for him. While no one can fill the shoes of another, I'm honored to follow in his footsteps.

TOP AND OPPOSITE: *An estimated 1,500 guests—including former presidents Bush, Clinton, and Carter and other dignitaries—attended the dedication of the Billy Graham Library in Charlotte, North Carolina on May 31, 2007. Styled after a* *dairy barn, the Library features historic displays and multimedia theaters that show the events and milestones of Billy's lifelong mission: to tell others about the love of Christ.*

ABOVE: *The BGEA headquarters in Charlotte, North Carolina*

"In the beginning we were just three or four simple people— we still are simple—who didn't know any better than to trust the Lord." ⁓ *Billy Graham*

THE BILLY GRAHAM EVANGELISTIC ASSOCIATION

Billy preached the Gospel to millions of people with the support of a dedicated team of prayer partners, financial supporters, staff, and a board of directors who comprise the BGEA. Together, this group of people—many who were Billy's close friends and longtime associates —continue to minister to the needs of millions of people each year. Billy was always grateful for their support and often commented on the BGEA's integral role in his life's work. "This ministry," he liked to explain to the crowds who attended his crusades, "is a team effort. Without their help, this ministry and all of our dreams to spread the Good News of God's love throughout the world would not have been possible."

The BGEA does more than just conduct crusades and festivals. It also offers help to millions of people who contact the organization each year. Ever since Billy first broadcast *The Hour of Decision* in 1950, people from all over the globe have written to the BGEA asking for guidance and prayer. In an effort to respond to the mountains of letters, the organization created a Spiritual Guidance department that consists of experienced pastors and counselors qualified to help people from all walks of life.

In 2002, after many years in Minneapolis, the BGEA moved its headquarters to Billy's birthplace of Charlotte, North Carolina. Two years earlier, Franklin had been selected by the BGEA board of directors to serve as chairman of the organization. Billy reflected on these changes, saying, "Over half a century ago, God led us to establish this organization as a tool in His hands, to reach the world for Christ by every means possible. With Franklin's leadership, BGEA will continue its calling of evangelism."

SAMARITAN'S PURSE

For more than twenty years, Franklin Graham has served as president and CEO of Samaritan's Purse, an international relief and evangelism organization that has cared for millions of suffering people in 115 countries, while sharing the Good News of God's love. Samaritan's Purse provides food, shelter, medical attention, and other assistance in all parts of the world, whether due to war, poverty, disease, or natural disasters. During one year alone, its medical department, World Medical Mission, placed 286 doctors and other medical personnel in twenty-one countries on five continents.

One of the ministry's projects, Operation Christmas Child, brings gifts to millions of children in eighty-six countries around the world. Volunteers in six countries pack simple shoe boxes with toys, candy, and other small gifts, and Samaritan's Purse brings them to children, providing relief from their daily suffering and dreary surroundings. In 2005, the ministry delivered more than seven million boxes with toys and booklets in their own languages that explained the true meaning of Christmas.

"Samaritan's Purse works with local churches and missionaries in strategic locations throughout the world to meet critical needs while sharing the Good News of Jesus Christ." ∽ *Franklin Graham*

TOP: *Franklin visited an orphanage that Samaritan's Purse supports in Hanoi, Vietnam, in 2000.*

ABOVE: *During wartime in 1995, children in Bosnia received shoe boxes filled with* toys, candy, and other small gifts through Operation Christmas Child.

LEFT AND OPPOSITE: *Franklin greeted the children of Honduras in 1998.*

FRANKLIN GRAHAM FESTIVALS

Franklin Graham began his work with BGEA as an associate evangelist, preaching his first crusade in March 1989 in Juneau, Alaska. Since that time, Franklin has held more than eighty crusades on five continents. In the early 1990s he changed the name of his meetings from crusades to festivals in order to attract a younger generation. "My generation," says Franklin, "is very familiar with 'festivals.' They attend music festivals, art festivals, balloon festivals, and so on. Therefore, in order to effectively reach these people, we offer a familiar setting with music from many top Christian artists and Grammy Award winners where people can hear about and respond to God's love for them."

"I have found that telling someone else the Good News of Jesus Christ is one of life's greatest privileges—for when someone really hears and believes the Gospel, his life is changed forever."

~ *Franklin Graham*

OPPOSITE: *An integrated crowd of forty-five thousand filled the stadium during a Franklin Graham festival in Cape Town, South Africa, 1997.*

TOP: *Franklin has preached the Good News at hundreds of festivals on five continents.*

MIDDLE AND RIGHT: *More than 132,000 people attended the three-day festival in Lima, Peru, in 1998.*

"I have been many places in the past few years where the masses of people are looking for some kind of savior to rescue them from the political and moral messes in which they find them-selves. Only a personal relationship with the living God can fill the moral vacuum that exists in the world today. It is God and God alone who can solve the crises in which we find ourselves, and He uses people to carry out His work." ∼ *Franklin Graham*

Thousands of people poured onto the stadium floor to accept Christ at a Franklin Graham festival in Asuncion, Paraguay, in 2005. Since 1989, Franklin has turned thousands to the Lord.

Billy in front of his Montreat home in 1993. Over the years, he and Ruth entertained everyone from Richard Nixon to Muhammed Ali on their humble front porch.

My Hope for You

Over the years, I have often been asked, "Do you have any hope for the future of the human race?" "Yes," I always reply. "I do have hope!" I don't think people can live without it. What oxygen is to our lungs, hope is to our survival in this world. And the Bible is filled with hope. God's Word tells us there is a divine Creator, a God who loves us and cares for each one of us.

I know there is a God. Although I cannot prove it scientifically, the evidence is overwhelming. I look out at the stars, the moon, and the sun. I watch the sun come up in the morning, and I know our planet is in perfect precision. The miracle of birth should be proof enough that something—Someone—beyond you and me must be behind all this.

But there is another reason I believe in God, and that is because God has revealed Himself to us! He did this in the person of Jesus Christ, whom the Bible calls "Immanuel," which means "God with us" (Matthew 1:23). Do you want to know what God is like? Look at Jesus Christ as He is revealed in the Gospels of the New Testament. By His life, death, and resurrection, Jesus demonstrated for all time that God loves us and that there can be hope as we open ourselves up to Him—hope for a new life now, and hope for life after death.

But you may say, "If God really loves us so much, why does He allow millions of people to starve in Third World countries? Why is there so much evil in our world?" To be honest, I can't always explain sin and suffering, nor can anyone else. There are some clues, though, as to the problem of pain. The Bible teaches that there is another power at work—the power of the devil. Satan is real and is opposed to everything God is doing. And we must never overlook the capacity for evil within the human heart.

When a society loses its moral and spiritual moorings, a vacuum is created, and inevitably we fall victim to violence, despair, false gods, and tyranny. Without God in our lives, no matter how far we advance scientifically, our hearts will remain exactly the same—ruled by sin. Human nature needs transforming so our hearts won't be controlled by hate, lust, and greed. We need new hearts—hearts filled with love and peace and joy.

Maybe you are feeling that need today. How many times have you wished that you could start over with a clean slate—with a new life? Perhaps you have tried everything else and have not found satisfaction. Resolve right now to allow God to wipe your slate clean by confessing your sins and asking Christ to give you a brand-new start.

The Bible says that only one thing will keep us out of heaven, and that is our sin. That is why we need to be forgiven and cleansed—and the only way that can happen is for God to do it. Jesus said, "I am the way and the truth and the life. No one comes to the Father except through me" (John 14:6). Many years ago as a teenager, I gave my life to Christ. From that moment on, I knew my sins were forgiven and that one day I would go to heaven. Christ also gave me a new purpose and a new joy in living that after more than seventy years, I still have. This can happen to you.

The Bible has much to say about the brevity of life and the necessity of preparing for eternity. I am convinced that only when we are prepared to die—both spiritually and emotionally—are we also prepared to live. Are you ready to surrender your life to Christ and to let go of your old ways? Ask Him to come into your heart and your life and to wash away your sins. He will forgive you. God loves you and knows what is best for you, and He wants you to be with Him forever in heaven. The Bible says, "For God so loved the world that he gave his one and only son, that whoever believes in him shall not perish but have eternal life" (John 3:16).

After a lifetime of ministry to people all over the world, I know this for sure: Jesus Christ makes life worth living. I have seen too many lives untangled and rehabilitated, too many homes reconstructed—too many people who have found peace and joy through a simple, humble confession of faith—to ever doubt that He is the answer. May this be your experience as well, as you turn to Christ in humility and faith, and open your life to His love and transforming power. I pray that you will make this important decision today.

God bless you,

"Someday you will read or hear that Billy Graham is dead. Don't you believe a word of it! I will just have changed my address. I will have gone into the presence of God." ∽ *Billy Graham*